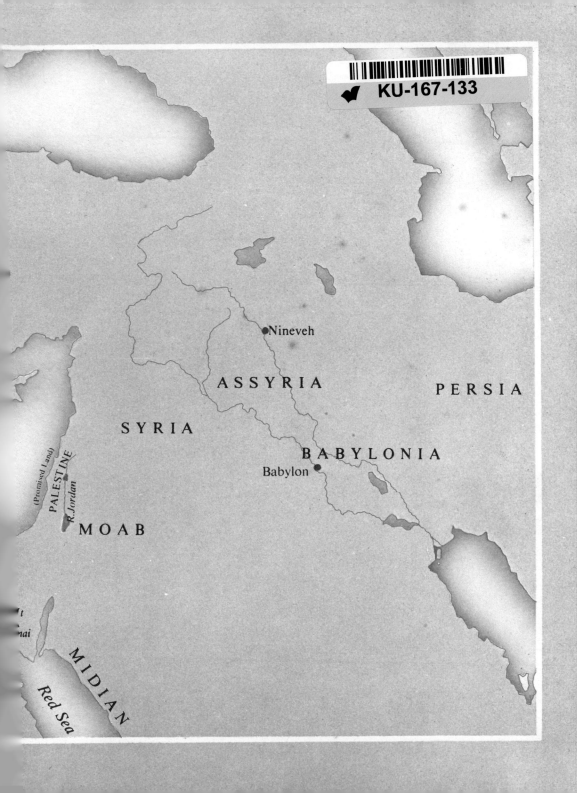

Nineveh

ASSYRIA

PERSIA

SYRIA

(Promised Land)
PALESTINE
R.Jordan

BABYLONIA

Babylon

MOAB

Sinai

MIDIAN

Red Sea

100 BIBLE STORIES

Retold by Norman J. Bull

Illustrated by Val Biro

HAMLYN
London · New York · Sydney · Toronto

Published 1980 by The Hamlyn Publishing Group Limited
London · New York · Sydney · Toronto
Astronaut House, Feltham, Middlesex, England
© Copyright The Hamlyn Publishing Group Limited 1980

ISBN 0 600 31580 0   Printed in Italy by Interlitho

Acknowledgements
Endpaper illustrations by Creative
Cartography Limited

Contents

8

In the beginning

In the beginning there was God. God made everything. For at first there were only waters and black darkness.

First God said: 'Let there be light.' And there was the light called day and the darkness called night.

Then God said: 'Let there be sky.' And there was the mighty arch of heaven.

Then God said: 'Let there be dry land.' And there was earth and the waters called seas.

Then God said: 'Let things grow in the earth.' And there were plants and trees.

Then God said: 'Let there be lights in heaven.' And there

was sun to lighten the day, moon to lighten the night, and twinkling stars in the sky.

Then God said: 'Let living things fill the sky and seas.' And the sky was filled with birds, and the seas were filled with fishes.

Then God said: 'Let there be living things on earth.' And there were animals and insects.

Then God said: 'Let there be people on earth.' And there were men and women. God made them just like himself to be his friends. God blessed them, saying: 'Fill the earth with children, and take care of all the animals.'

God had finished making heaven and earth. He looked down from heaven on all that he had made. And God saw that it was good.

The first mother and father

God made dry land rise up out of the waters. He called it earth. But nothing could live on its dry land. So God made a mist to water it, and dusty earth became soft clay. God used the soft clay to make the shape of a man. Then God breathed into him, and the man came alive. The name of this first man was Adam.

God made a home for Adam. It was the beautiful Garden of Eden, watered by a great river, filled with trees and plants and flowers. The soil was soft and rich, and Adam lived there happily, growing crops for food.

But God said: 'It is not good for Adam to be alone. He needs a friend and helper.' Then God made Adam fall asleep. He took a rib-bone out of Adam's body, and healed the place. From the rib he made a woman and brought her to Adam.

Adam was delighted to have a wife. He called her Eve, and loved her dearly. His seed passed into her, making the egg inside her a living child. Three children were born to Adam and Eve. From them came more and more children.

So Adam was the father of mankind, and Eve was the mother of all people on earth.

Noah and his ark

God had made Adam and Eve so that they could fill the earth with people. God wanted people to be his friends. They would be kind, and loving, and good.

But God began to feel sorry for what he had done. 'People on earth are full of evil,' he said to himself. 'They are bad, and wicked, and cruel. There is only one good man – my servant Noah. He alone is kind and loving. I will rid the earth of people, except for Noah and his family. Then I can make a fresh start, with only good people on earth.'

Then God said to Noah: 'The earth will be flooded with

waters. Build an ark of strong wood. Cover it with pitch to keep out the water. Take your family into the ark, and take two of every kind of animal. Then I can make a fresh start.'

Noah did as God commanded. He made his ark strong and safe. He took all his family and two of every kind of animal into the ark. Then came the floods. First the land was covered with water, then the hills, then even the mountains. Every living thing on earth was drowned in the floods.

But Noah and his family and the animals were safe in the ark. God would make a fresh start with them.

The rainbow sign

For forty days the rains poured down. The whole earth was under the waters. But Noah's ark rode safely on top of the waters.

At last the rains stopped, but it was many days before the waters began to go down. Noah sent out a dove. It fluttered back wearily, for there was nothing to rest on. Again he sent out a dove. It came back with an olive-leaf in its beak. Again he sent out a dove. It never came back. Now Noah knew that the earth was dry again.

Noah went out of the ark on to dry land. At once he made a holy place to worship God.

God spoke there to Noah: 'I give my blessing to you and your sons. Fill the earth with children. Care for the animals and trees and plants. Follow my ways, and I will always be your God.'

Then God made a solemn promise: 'Never again will the earth be covered with waters. There will always be seed-time and harvest, cold and heat, summer and winter, day and night. This is the sign that I will keep my promise – I will set my bow of many colours in the sky. When rain clouds appear in the sky my rainbow will appear also. It will be a sign for ever of my promise to all mankind.'

Abraham the great father

God called a man named Abraham. 'Leave your home and your country,' God said. 'I will lead you into a new land. I will be your God and will bless you.' Abraham trusted God. He took Sarah his wife, his family, his servants, his sheep and goats, and set out into a strange country.

Abraham and his family were wanderers. They stopped wherever there was water for the animals.

Again God appeared to Abraham and said: 'Lift up your eyes over all this land. I promise it to you and your children.'

Again God appeared to Abraham and said: 'Lift up your eyes to the stars in the sky. Can you count them? No, they are too many. I promise you that one day the people born from you will be just as many. I have named you Abraham which means great father, for you will be the great father of many people. I am your God. I will be their God.'

Abraham trusted God. But he was worried. He was growing old, and no children had been born to him and Sarah. God kept his promise and Sarah bore Abraham a little son. They named him Isaac which means laughter, for they were happy. Now Abraham could be the father of many people.

Isaac and Rebecca

Father Abraham was very old when his son Isaac became a man. He must choose a wife for Isaac, so that his family could go on and become the people of God. He sent his faithful steward back to his own people to choose a wife for Isaac.

It was evening when the steward came to the people of Abraham. He stopped by the well. Soon the girls would be coming out to draw water. He prayed to God to help him choose a wife for Isaac. He would ask for water for himself. The girl who offered water for his camels too would be the one God had chosen.

A beautiful girl came and filled her pitcher with water. The steward went to her and begged for a drink.

'Drink, my lord,' she said. 'I will draw water for your camels too.' Then the steward knew that she was the one God had chosen. Her name was Rebecca.

Rebecca's father gave his blessing to the marriage. Rebecca herself was willing to go at once. Early the next morning they set out.

Isaac was in the fields when he saw the camels coming. He hurried to Rebecca, and loved her dearly. Soon Isaac and Rebecca were married, and they lived together in great happiness.

Jacob and his dream

Isaac and Rebecca had two sons named Esau and Jacob. When they grew up Esau became a hunter, and Jacob looked after the sheep and goats. One day the brothers had a quarrel. Jacob cheated Esau, and his brother sought to kill him. Jacob had to flee to save his life.

That night Jacob slept in a lonely rocky place and
dreamt. In his dream he saw a ladder reaching up to
heaven. Angels of God were passing up and down. He saw
God himself, standing above, and heard his voice: 'I am the
God of your grandfather Abraham, and of your father Isaac.
I am with you. I will guard you and bless you. Your children
will be as many as the dust of the earth. From you will come
my chosen people.'

When Jacob awoke he said: 'Truly, God is in this place! It
is the very gate of heaven!' Jacob made a holy place there. And
he made a solemn promise: 'If my fathers' God will be with
me he shall be my God, too.'

Jacob went away to dwell with the people of his mother
Rebecca. He had many sons. He became rich and great.
After many years he came back to the Promised Land. Esau
went to meet him. The brothers wept with joy at being
together again.

Joseph and his dreams

Jacob had twelve sons. His favourite was young Joseph. When Joseph was seventeen years old he went out to join his elder brothers, looking after the sheep. His brothers wore short coats with no sleeves, so that their arms and legs were free for hard work. Jacob had a special coat made for Joseph, with fine colours. It was a long coat with sleeves. It showed that Joseph was a master, not just a common worker like his brothers. This made them jealous of Joseph, and they began to hate him.

Joseph had fine dreams and he could tell what they meant. One day he said to his brothers: 'I dreamed that we were binding sheaves of corn at harvest time. My sheaf stood up tall and straight. All your sheaves bowed down to mine.'

'What!' cried his brothers. 'Does this mean that you're going to lord it over us?' And they hated Joseph even more.

Joseph told them another dream, with the same meaning. He told his father too.

Jacob said: 'Does this mean that your mother and I and all your brothers will bow down to you, my son?'

Jacob could see that Joseph would become a wise man. But his brothers hated him, and they wanted to get rid of him.

Joseph becomes a slave

One day Jacob sent Joseph to visit his brothers, far away with the sheep. They saw his coat of many colours a long way off.

'Here comes the dreamer!' they cried. 'Let's kill him, and throw his body into a pit! We'll say that a wild animal seized him.'

'No,' said Reuben, the eldest, 'let's throw him into a pit and

23

leave him to die.' Reuben hoped to save Joseph from death, and to rescue him later.

When Joseph came they tore off his coat, and put him in a deep pit, dug in the ground. Then they sat down to eat. Now some merchants came by, their camels loaded with spices to sell in Egypt.

'Let's sell Joseph to the merchants,' said one brother. 'Then we need not kill him. After all, he is our brother.' They all agreed.

So they sold Joseph to the merchants as a slave. Then they dipped Joseph's coat in the blood of a goat. 'Look, father!' they cried when they got back. 'Isn't this the coat you gave to Joseph?'

'It is my son's coat! A wild beast must have seized him! Oh Joseph, my dear, dear son,' Jacob sobbed.

No one could comfort Jacob, for he believed that Joseph was dead. But Joseph was alive – a slave in Egypt.

Joseph in prison

The merchants sold Joseph as a slave in Egypt. He was
bought by Potiphar, captain of the Royal Guard. He soon
found that Joseph was a wise man. He put Joseph in charge of
his household. But his wife told lies about Joseph, and
Potiphar sent him to the royal prison.

The keeper of the prison found how wise Joseph was, too.
He put Joseph in charge of the prisoners. Among them were
the butler and baker of Pharaoh, the king. One morning they
both looked sad. 'Each of us had a dream,' they told Joseph.
'But we don't know what they mean.'

'My God has made me wise,' said Joseph. 'I can tell you the
meaning of your dreams.'

'In my dream,' said the butler, 'I saw a vine with three
bunches of grapes. I pressed them into Pharaoh's cup, and
gave the cup of wine into his hand.'

'The three bunches are three days,' said Joseph. 'In three
days Pharaoh will forgive you, and you will be serving him
with wine again.' But the baker's dream meant that in three
days he would die.

Three days later Pharaoh had his baker put to death. He
forgave his butler. But the butler soon forgot all about
Joseph. Joseph lay in prison for two more years.

Joseph the ruler of Egypt

One night Pharaoh, King of Egypt, dreamt that he stood by
the river. Seven fat cows came out of the water and chewed

grass in the meadow. Then seven thin cows came out of the water. They ate up the seven fat cows, but they were just as thin as before! Whatever did it mean?

Pharaoh was very worried. None of his wise men could explain his dream. Then his butler remembered Joseph, and told Pharaoh. He sent for Joseph. 'I hear that you are wise and can explain dreams,' Pharaoh said.

'It is not me,' said Joseph. 'My God speaks through me.' Then Pharaoh told his dream and Joseph explained it.

'God has shown you what is to come, Pharaoh. There will be seven fat years with plenty of food. Then there will be seven thin years of hunger, when people will forget the fat years of plenty. Let Pharaoh set a wise man to rule over Egypt. He can store food in the years of plenty and so have food for the years of hunger.'

Then Pharaoh said: 'Truly your God has filled you with wisdom. I will set you to rule over all Egypt. Here is my ring to show that you rule for me.'

Then Joseph rode through Egypt in the royal chariot. The people bowed down before Joseph the ruler of Egypt.

Joseph welcomes his family

For seven years there was plenty of food. Joseph stored up corn all over the land of Egypt. Then came seven years without rain. There was hunger in many lands, except Egypt, and people went down to Egypt to buy corn. Among them were the elder brothers of Joseph.

Joseph knew his brothers at once. But they did not recognise Joseph. Joseph accused them of being spies. He kept one brother back and sent the others to fetch the youngest brother, Benjamin, to prove that they came from the place they had said. It was a trick so that Joseph could see his dear brother Benjamin.

On the next trip they brought Benjamin but, before they went home, Joseph had his silver cup hidden in Benjamin's sack. The brothers were brought back for stealing. Benjamin was ordered to stay in Egypt as a slave.

'That would break the heart of our father Jacob,' said one brother. 'Please take me instead.'

Then Joseph could hide his secret no longer. With tears of joy he told his brothers who he was. He bade them hurry home, and bring back Jacob with them.

So Jacob and his whole family came to Egypt, and Joseph welcomed them with tears of happiness. The people of God dwelt in Egypt for many years.

29

Baby Moses

The people of God lived happily in Egypt for many years.
They had many children, and their numbers grew. But then
came a new Pharaoh who feared these strangers. 'Make them
slaves,' he ordered. 'They can build new cities for me.
Stand over them with whips.' Their lives were hard and
bitter. But still they grew in number. Then Pharaoh made a
new order against them: 'Every baby boy must be drowned in
the river.'

A certain woman had a baby boy. She made a little ark
with bulrushes, covered it with pitch to keep it dry, and put
her baby inside. She hid the ark in the bulrushes growing in
the water. Her little daughter stayed near to watch.

A princess came to the river to bathe. She saw the ark, and
sent a maid to fetch it. She felt sorry for the crying baby.

The baby's sister said: 'Shall I fetch a slave lady to nurse it for you?'

'Yes,' said the princess. So the girl fetched her mother.

'Nurse this baby for me and I will pay you,' the princess said to her. So the baby was looked after by his own mother.

When he was a young boy she brought him back to the princess. The princess made him her son, and named him Moses. So Moses was saved from death, and grew up in a royal palace.

God calls Moses

Moses grew up in a royal palace, but he never forgot his own people. When he became a man he was angry to see them toiling as slaves. One day he saw an Egyptian hitting a slave. Moses was so angry that he killed the Egyptian. When he knew that he had been found out he had to flee from Egypt.

Moses fled to the land of Midian. He became the shepherd of Jethro, a holy man. He married the daughter of Jethro and settled in the land of Midian.

One day Moses was seeking water for his sheep. He came near to a holy mountain called Sinai. The hot sun glittered on a bush and seemed to set it alight – but it did not burn away. Moses came near to see the wonder, and there God spoke to him: 'Moses! I am the God of your fathers. This is my holy mountain. Go back to Egypt, and save my people from their slavery. Tell them I sent you. Lead them out of Egypt, and bring them here to me.'

Moses was afraid, but God made him brave. He went back to Egypt, and told the slaves how God had sent him. Then they bowed their heads, and worshipped the God of their fathers.

Moses the leader

God gave Moses the courage to go back to Egypt. Moses spoke bravely to Pharaoh: 'God says, "Let my people go!"'

'No. They must work harder than ever,' Pharaoh ordered. The people were angry with Moses for making things worse for them.

'God will save you,' Moses promised.

Then horrors came upon the land of Egypt. First the river turned red. Then came frogs; then insects; then thunderstorms; then locusts; then sandstorms. Everyone believed that these were signs from God. But Pharaoh's heart was hard. He would not let the slaves go.

Then came a sickness among the children. Many of them died, even the eldest son of Pharaoh. Pharaoh was afraid, and he let the slaves go.

Moses led the slaves out of Egypt. The Sea of Reeds lay before them, and they could not cross. Then they heard the thunder of horses' hooves behind them. Pharaoh had changed his mind, and sent soldiers in chariots to bring the slaves back. There was no hope for them.

Then suddenly a fierce wind arose and drove back the waters. There was dry land and the people hurried across. The horsemen galloped after them. But the wind dropped, the waters rolled back, and their chariots were stuck in the mud. So the people of God were saved from slavery in Egypt.

34

Moses the law-giver

Moses led the people to the sacred mountain of Sinai where God had called him. The holy mountain was a fearful sight. It was a volcano and its top was hidden in dark clouds, red with fire. Only Moses, God's chosen leader, could climb up and come close to God. There God gave laws for his people. Moses wrote them on two tablets of stone, and brought them down to the people.

On one tablet were laws telling the people their duty to God. They must not worship other gods. They must not worship idols of wood or stone. They must keep God's name holy. They must keep God's day holy. They must honour their parents.

On the other tablet were laws telling the people their duty to each other. They must not kill. They must not steal the wife or husband of someone else. They must not steal anything belonging to someone else. They must not tell lies about others. They must not want anything belonging to someone else.

These were the ten commandments which God gave to his people through Moses. At the sacred mountain of Sinai the people made their solemn promise to live by these laws from God. He was their God and they were his chosen people.

Joshua the leader

Moses led the people of God to the land which God had promised to Abraham. He sent out spies, and they said: 'It is a land flowing with milk and honey.' But people lived there in strong towns, with mighty walls. It would be hard to win the Promised Land.

The people of God had a beautiful Ark, or chest, made of fine wood and covered with gold. Inside it were the two stone tablets of the laws given to Moses. On the lid were two golden angels. When the Ark was with them the people knew that God was with them. He would lead them into the Promised Land.

When Moses died, the people chose Joshua to be their

36

new leader, as Moses had advised.

God said to him: 'Be strong and brave. I have promised this land to you. I will always be with you.'

Joshua led the people across the River Jordan and into the Promised Land. They faced the strong town of Jericho. The Ark was carried round and round its high walls to show that Jericho belonged to the people of God. Then they attacked the town and took it.

Joshua captured another town named Shiloh. There a temple was built as a home for the Ark. The people went to Shiloh to worship God, and to thank him for leading them into the Promised Land.

Gideon the warrior

Many of the people of God became farmers in the
Promised Land. There they had new enemies called
Midianites. They were desert wanderers, riding on fast
camels. They raided the farms for food. They destroyed the
crops, and killed the animals, while the frightened farmers hid
in caves.

   God called Gideon, a farmer's son, to lead his people.
Gideon called men to join him, and thousands came. But
Gideon wanted only a few good fighters. 'You face many
dangers if you join me!' he threatened. Lots of men slunk
away: but there were still too many.

'Come and drink at the river before we fight,' Gideon
ordered. Many men got on their knees, and bent their heads
to drink. Gideon sent these careless men back home. Only
three hundred men lifted water in their hands to their mouths,
keeping their eyes alert and watchful. They were the men he
wanted.

Gideon made a night attack on the camp of the sleeping
Midianites. Each man had a trumpet, and a lighted torch
hidden in a jug. Then Gideon gave the signal. The three
hundred men blew their trumpets, broke their jugs, held
their lamps high, and burst into the camp. The Midianites
thought it was a huge army, and they fled in terror. Never
again did the Midianites trouble the people of God.

The call of Samuel

One day a lady named Hannah brought her little son Samuel to the temple at Shiloh. Hannah told Eli the priest how she had promised God that, if he gave her a son, he would be a man of God. 'I am keeping my promise,' she said.

Samuel was very happy living at the temple. He helped Eli to watch over the sacred Ark, to keep the lamps burning, and to care for the little wooden temple. Once a year his mother came, bringing Samuel a new coat that she had made for him.

One night Samuel lay on his mattress, going off to sleep, when he heard a voice calling him: 'Samuel! Samuel!'

He ran to Eli. 'I didn't call you, my son. Go back to bed.'

Again he heard the voice, and again he ran to Eli. When he came a third time, Eli knew that it was God calling Samuel. He said: 'If you hear the voice again, say, "Speak, Lord. Your servant is listening."'

Samuel did just as Eli told him. And God spoke to Samuel in the silence of the night. Then Eli knew that God had called Samuel to lead his people.

When Samuel grew up he travelled through the land each year. All the people of God honoured him as the man of God.

Samuel chooses Saul

Samuel, the man of God, was worried. Strong enemies called Philistines were attacking the people of God, and seizing the Promised Land. They needed a warrior to lead them in battle. 'I must give them a king,' Samuel decided. But whom should he choose?

One day a tall, strong young man named Saul came up to Samuel in the market-place of his town, to seek his help. Samuel knew at once that Saul was the man to choose. After they had talked he told Saul to kneel down, anointed his head with holy oil, and said: 'In the name of God I appoint you king over his people.' Not long after, the people gathered together and Saul was hailed as king with great rejoicing.

Saul soon raised an army, and fought well against their enemies. But he became proud and hard. He would not obey Samuel, and he even tried to cheat him.

Samuel spoke sternly to Saul: 'You have rebelled against God. Instead of being sorry you are hard and proud. You have turned away from God; now God has turned away from you.'

Samuel left King Saul and never saw him again. He felt sorry for Saul. But he knew, now, that he must find another king for the people of God.

Samuel chooses David

God called Samuel to go to the little town of Bethlehem. A farmer named Jesse lived there. God had chosen one of his sons to be king.

Samuel led the people of Bethlehem in the worship of God. Then he asked Jesse: 'Which is your eldest son?' The

43

eldest son was brought to him. 'No, he's not the one,' said
Samuel. Jesse brought his second son. 'No, he's not the one,'
said Samuel. Jesse brought seven of his sons, one by one. But
Samuel knew in his heart that God had chosen none of them.

Now Samuel was worried. 'Are these all your sons?' he
asked.

'Why yes,' said Jesse, 'except for David, the youngest. He
looks after the sheep.'

'Send for him,' Samuel ordered. 'We will not sit down to eat
till he comes.'

At last David was brought in, a strong, handsome young
man with fine eyes. At once Samuel knew that David was the
one God had chosen. He anointed the head of David with his
holy oil. So David was to be the new king.

But the anointing had to be kept secret, for fear of King
Saul. So David went back to be with his sheep on the hills of
Bethlehem.

David the shepherd boy

David loved being with his sheep. He knew the name of each
one and they all knew his voice. He looked after them all day,
and guarded them all night.

David led them out in the morning, and found grass for
them to nibble. When the sun grew hot he found cool water
for them and shade from the sun. They were frightened by
running water, so he found still waters. There they rested.

Towards evening David led them to the fold, with walls of
stone, where they were safe from wild beasts. Then he lay
across the way into the fold. He himself was the door. The
sheep were safe for the night.

David always carried his shepherd's tools. He had his staff,
a tall stick with a curve at one end for lifting a sheep. He had

his thick club, to beat off wild beasts. He had his horn of oil,
for bathing cuts and scratches. He had his water-bottle and a
satchel for his food. He had his sling for hurling stones and his
harp for playing songs.

One day David made up a new song. It began: 'The Lord is
my Shepherd.' It told how God cared for his people, just as
David cared for his sheep.

David and his harp

David loved making music with his harp, as he sat with his sheep. It was made of hard cypress wood. Its eight strings were made of sheep-gut. It was quite small and easy to carry and to play with one hand.

David had plenty of time to play. He made up songs of his own, and sang them as his hand plucked the strings. He became famous for his songs.

One day a servant came out to look after the sheep. David must hurry back home, for he was wanted urgently. His father told him sad news. King Saul had become worse. His fits of anger, when anyone crossed him, were turning into fits of madness. Only music could sooth him. His servants were looking everywhere for a fine harp-player. They had heard of David and his music. They needed him for King Saul.

So David went to the fortress where King Saul lived. Each day he sat with the king, making sweet and gentle music to sooth his madness. King Saul grew to love the shepherd boy from Bethlehem, who could bring peace and calm to his troubled mind.

David and his sling

Each day David practised with his sling. It was made from a piece of goatskin. It was narrow at each end, and wide in the middle. There was a hollow in the middle for a smooth round pebble. A leather string was tied to each end.

David aimed at a tree some way off. There were plenty of pebbles by the water. He put one in his sling and held it by the two strings. He whirled it round and round his head. Then he let one string go and the pebble flew to its target. David scored a perfect hit every time.

David walked in front of his sheep. Sometimes, when he

looked round, he saw that a lamb had wandered off. Then David hurled a pebble. It landed exactly in front of the lamb's nose, so that it was startled and ran back to the flock.

David's sling was a fine weapon, too. Sometimes a wild beast came after his sheep. There were hyenas, jackals, wolves, lions, bears. When David saw one in the distance he let fly with his sling. He had killed a lion and a bear with his deadly shots.

David had no fear. For he believed that God watched over him, just as he watched over his sheep.

49

David and Goliath

The brothers of David were soldiers in the army of King Saul. One day his father sent him to take some food to them.

The soldiers of King Saul faced the army of the Philistines, their armour glittering in the sun. While David was there the Philistines sent out their champion named Goliath. He was a giant of a man. 'Send out your champion to fight me!' he roared to the soldiers of King Saul. 'We'll decide the battle between the two of us!'

The soldiers of King Saul were terrified.

'I'll go and fight him!' said David boldly.

They laughed at him. 'You're only a boy,' they said. 'You know nothing about fighting.'

'I killed a lion and a bear when I was guarding my sheep,' David said boldly.

David went out towards Goliath. The giant roared with laughter and mocked him. David picked smooth pebbles from the brook. He put one in his sling, whirled it round his head, and let fly. The stone hit Goliath right on his forehead, and the giant fell down unconscious. David ran to him, pulled out Goliath's sword, and killed him.

When the Philistines saw that their champion was dead they fled away, chased by the soldiers of King Saul. David had won the battle for the people of God.

David in hiding

David became a fine soldier, and King Saul made him commander of his army. David was handsome, brave, and popular with the people. They sang the praises of David, instead of praising Saul. The king grew mad with jealousy.

One day, as David played his harp to soothe Saul, the King seized his spear and hurled it at David. So David fled for his life.

David had to hide from the king. He and his men lived in a cave. For Saul and his men were seeking everywhere for David so that they could kill him.

One night, King Saul and his guard came into the cave, and lay down to sleep.

'God has delivered him into your hands,' David's men whispered.

'No!' said David. 'He is the anointed king.' David cut off a piece of the king's robe. When dawn came the king and his guard awoke and went out.

David followed them and called: 'My lord king! See this piece of your robe! I could have killed you. But I am your loyal servant. Why do you hate me, and seek to kill me?' And Saul wept in his madness.

Soon after, King Saul had to face the Philistines in battle. His army was beaten, and Saul died. David wept in bitter grief for the king.

David the king

When David was a boy he had been anointed by Samuel, the
man of God. Now that Saul was dead the people gladly took
David as king. In time he ruled over all the people of God.

When the Philistines heard that David was king they
marched against him. David defeated them in battle, and
drove them back to their own land. Never again did they
attack the people of God. David conquered other lands too,
and made a fine kingdom for his people.

David needed a capital city. He chose a strong fortress in
the middle of his kingdom, high on a hill. It was called
Jerusalem. David's men climbed up the underground tunnel
which brought water into the fortress. They took the people
by surprise, opened the gates, and David's soldiers rushed in
to capture the fortress. So Jerusalem became the City of
David.

David was king of the people of God for over thirty years.
He was a wise ruler, and his people loved their popular king.
His reign was so happy that the people of God never forgot it.
It was their golden age, the best time they ever had.

The City of David

King David had captured the fortress of Jerusalem, and made it his capital city. He had his royal court at Jerusalem, and there he ruled over his fine kingdom.

But it was not just the City of David. He wanted to make it the City of God, where God dwelt among his chosen people. So the sacred Ark must be brought to Jerusalem. It was the Golden Ark which had led the people of God into the Promised Land. Inside it were the stone tablets on which Moses had written the laws of God. When the Ark was with them the people knew that God was with them.

David sent for the Ark of God. It was brought to Jerusalem with great rejoicing. The trumpets sounded, the musicians played, the choirs sang. David was so happy and excited that he too joined in the dancing, as the people shouted with joy. Then the Ark was placed in a special tent, until the time came to build a temple to be its home.

So the City of David became the City of God. Still today Jerusalem is called the holy city. Pilgrims still go to worship God in Jerusalem, the City of David.

David and his sons

King David had many sons, and he loved them dearly. But when David was old they became rivals. For only one of them could be king after their father.

Absalom, one of David's sons, even plotted against his father. He raised an army to make himself king. When David heard the sad news he left Jerusalem, so that the city would not be attacked. He gave strict orders to his soldiers: 'Beware that no one hurts Absalom.'

During the battle, in a wood, Absalom rode his mule under an oak tree. His long hair caught in its thick branches. The mule went on, leaving Absalom hanging there, and he could not free himself. Soldiers of David found their enemy hanging there, and they killed Absalom.

David waited anxiously for news of the battle. His men
were afraid to tell him. When David heard he wept bitterly.
'O Absalom, my son, my son', he cried. 'Would to God I had
died rather than you.'

Another son tried to become king, too. But David had
decided that his son Solomon should be king after him. So
Solomon was anointed at a gathering of the people. The
trumpets were blown, and all the people cried: 'God save
King Solomon!'

57

Solomon and his dream

When David died his son Solomon became king. One night he had a dream. God appeared to him and said: 'Ask for what you want most, and I will give it to you.'

The king said: 'I have many people to rule over, and I know so little. Make me wise, so that I know what is good for my people.'

God was pleased. He said: 'You could have asked to have a long life, or to be rich, or to conquer your enemies. Instead, you have asked to be wise. I am giving you a wise heart, so that you will serve your people well. I also give you the things you did not ask for – a long life, and riches, and victory over your enemies. Keep my commandments, just as your father David did, and I will give you all these things.'

So Solomon became a wise king. His clever sayings, called proverbs, were written down by his wise men in their books. Solomon made poems and songs, too. He became famous for his wisdom among his own people. His fame spread to other lands, and visitors came to the Promised Land to hear the wise king of the people of God.

Solomon the wise

One day two women came to King Solomon with a baby boy. One of them said: 'My lord, this woman and I live in the same house. I gave birth to a baby boy. Three days later this woman gave birth to a baby boy. There was no one else in the house. This woman's baby died in the night. So she came to my room, took my baby while I was asleep, and put her dead child in its place. When I woke to feed the baby I knew at once that it was not my child.'

The other woman said: 'No! This living baby is mine. The dead child was hers.'

Solomon turned to his officer. 'Fetch a sword,' he said. 'Now, cut the child in half, and give half to each woman.'

One woman said: 'Yes, that's fair.' But the other woman threw herself at the king's feet.

'No! No!' she cried. 'Don't kill the baby! Let her have it!' Solomon looked down at her, pleading for the child's life.

'This is the real mother,' he said. 'Give her the child. It is her son.'

This story spread far and wide. And all the people knew that God had blessed King Solomon with his wisdom.

Solomon in all his glory

King Solomon had been left a fine kingdom by his father David. So he did not have to fight wars. Instead he became famous for his glory.

Solomon had a great army, with hundreds of chariots and horses. The ships of his fine navy sailed down the Red Sea to trade with other lands. They brought back gold and silver, apes and peacocks, ivory and spices. Caravans of camels crossed the desert to bring precious goods like myrrh and incense to the royal court.

Solomon built a fine palace for himself at Jerusalem, where his guests drank from golden cups. The fame of his glory spread to other lands. One day there came to his court a queen from Sheba, the land of spices, in Arabia. She brought costly gifts for the great King Solomon – gold, and spices, and precious stones.

The Queen of Sheba was amazed at the glory, and splendour, and wisdom of Solomon. 'All that I heard is true,' she said. 'Now I know that your wisdom and glory are even greater than I had been told. Happy are your people to hear your wisdom. Blessed be your God who has made you so wise, so glorious, and so great.'

The temple of Solomon

King David had brought the sacred Ark of God to Jerusalem. Now his son Solomon built a beautiful temple for its home.

Builders came from the land of Phoenicia. Cypress and cedar trees were brought by sea. Blocks of stone were cut out of the hills. Copper was dug from the mines to make

bronze. Gold and silver were brought by ships from other lands. Then came seven years of building.

Doors were made of bronze. Walls were made of cedar wood, carved with flowers and trees. Holy tables made of wood were covered with gold, with golden candlesticks upon them. The home for the sacred Ark was the holy of holies, where the Ark's golden angels would glow in the darkness.

The great day came when the sacred Ark was to be taken to its new home. Trumpets blared, cymbals clashed, choirs sang. Shouts of praise and joy rose up as the procession moved towards the temple. Last of all came King Solomon in all his glory. He turned to face the people. In the hush he told them that God had come to dwell among them in the temple. Then he led them in prayer that God would always bless his house and his people who worshipped him there.

Elijah
the champion of God

King Ahab married a princess, named Jezebel, from another land. He built a new palace for her in the town of Jezreel. It had a lovely garden, but there was no space for growing herbs. Just outside was a small vineyard. It belonged to a poor man named Naboth.

King Ahab said to him: 'I need your vineyard to make a herb garden. I will pay you well.'

But Naboth said: 'I cannot let you have it. My father left it to me. I must leave it to my son.'

When Ahab told Jezebel, she said angrily, 'Aren't you the king? I'll get the vineyard of Naboth for you!'

Jezebel sent a letter to the chief men of Jezreel, written in the king's name. 'Put Naboth on trial,' the letter ordered. 'Pay men to say that he spoke against God and against the king. See that he is found guilty and put to death.' The chief men of Jezreel did as the letter ordered.

'Good news!' Jezebel said to Ahab when she heard. 'Naboth is dead! His vineyard is yours!'

King Ahab hurried eagerly down through the garden to Naboth's vineyard. There on the path stood Elijah, the man of God.

'God has sent me!' said Elijah sternly. 'You and your queen have done a great evil. God will punish you and your family for your wickedness.'

Then the king felt guilty, and showed his sorrow. For he knew in his heart that the people of God must deal justly with each other.

Elisha and the lady of Shunem

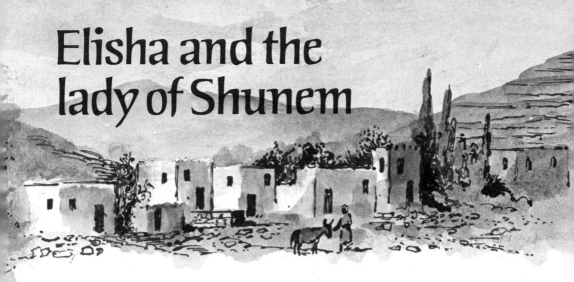

Elisha, the man of God, travelled through the land with his servant. He was a friend to everyone. He often passed through a town called Shunem. A rich lady of Shunem invited him into her house, and he often had food there on his journeys.

One day the lady said to her husband: 'Let's build a little room for the man of God on the flat roof of our house. Then he will have a place to sleep on his visits.' So they made a little room for him on the house-top. It had a bed, a table, a stool, and a candlestick. Elisha stayed there on his travels.

Elisha wanted to thank the lady for her kindness.

His servant said: 'She is rich and needs nothing. But she longs for a child.'

Then Elisha called her and said: 'God will bless you with a child.' And the lady of Shunem was blessed with a baby boy.

One day the little boy was out in the hot sun at harvest-time, watching the reapers. He became ill with sun-stroke. He was carried home, and lay as if he were dead. The lady hastened to find Elisha. He came gladly, and restored her son to life. Once again she gave thanks for the blessings brought by the kindly man of God.

Elisha and the little maid

There was war between the people of God and the people of the land called Syria. The army of Syria was led by General Naaman. His soldiers attacked the Promised Land. They took prisoners back to Syria. Among them was a little girl named Rebecca. General Naaman took her to be a servant for his wife.

One day General Naaman found that he had a disease of his skin called leprosy. No one could cure it. He would have to give up everything, and live alone till he died. Rebecca often found her mistress weeping bitterly in her room. She felt so sorry. 'If only my master went to my land,' Rebecca said, 'there is a man of God, called Elisha, who could heal him.'

Then General Naaman went back to the Promised Land. His chariot was full of rich presents for the man of God.

When he came to Elisha's house the servant told him: 'My master says, "Go and wash seven times in the river Jordan."' When Naaman came up out of the water his skin was pure and his body was whole again. Elisha would not take any presents. He did not want a reward for serving God.

Naaman hurried back home. What rejoicing there was! How glad Rebecca was to see her mistress happy again!

Amos the shepherd

Amos the shepherd lived quietly and simply with his sheep. But three times each year he went to the towns to sell his wool. He was horrified by what he saw there.

Traders had become rich. They lived in fine houses, feasting on costly food and drink. In the markets they cheated with the weights, put up the prices, and sold bad food.

They lent money to the poor. When the poor man could not pay they seized his land. They even sold his family as slaves. If the poor man went to court to get justice the rich man always won. He simply gave money to the judge. Holy men were as bad as rich men and judges. But they all went to church and thought God was pleased with them.

'How God must hate all this wrong-doing,' Amos thought to himself. 'He must be calling me to speak to the people for him.'

So Amos went to the town of Bethel, a holy place. 'God hates your evil ways!' he cried to the people. 'He will punish you! Don't think going to church will save you – he hates that too, for you do not live by his ways.'

Amos taught that God is just and fair. Only those who are just and fair to each other can be the people of God.

Hosea the baker

Hosea worked for a baker. He married Gomer, the daughter of his master. They lived together happily, and they had three children. Hosea loved his quiet family life at home.

But Gomer grew tired of it. She wanted fun and excitement. One day she put on her best clothes and her jewels, and went off to have a good time in the city.

Hosea's friends said: 'You're well rid of her! Divorce her, and find another wife.' But Hosea was heart-broken. He still loved Gomer. How could he give her up? He must go after her – yes, that was what God wanted.

Hosea went from town to town till he found Gomer, and brought her back home. He pleaded with her to be faithful to him and their children. But again and again Gomer went off, breaking his heart.

Hosea had to bring up their children by himself. He fed them, and clothed them, and taught them to walk. But it seems that they left Hosea, too, as soon as they could.

What a sad life Hosea had. But it taught him something new about God. God loved his people – just as Hosea loved Gomer. God could not give up his people – just as Hosea could not give up Gomer. For God is love.

Micah the peasant

Micah lived in a small country village, with other poor peasants. Each peasant had a piece of land to grow food for his family. But when the harvest was bad he had to borrow money to buy food. He had to pay back much more money than he borrowed. When he could not pay, the money-lender took his land, and even sold him and his family as slaves.

So the money-lenders grew rich. They lived in fine houses, with plenty of good food and drink, while poor peasants starved.

Micah was a fiery man, with a fierce love of God. How God must hate all this evil. He was just, so his people should be just and fair to each other. He must punish their wickedness.

Micah had to speak out. 'God is angry with you!' he cried to the people of Jerusalem. 'He will punish you! Your city will be destroyed.'

'Rubbish,' said the people. 'God is with us in his temple. No harm can come to our holy city.'

'Fools!' Micah shouted. 'Your city will be destroyed because of your evil!' His fiery words were remembered years later, when Jerusalem was being attacked.

Micah's words were written down, and we can still read his message to the people: 'God wants you to be just, and loving, and to walk humbly in his ways.'

Isaiah saves Jerusalem

Everyone was afraid of the Assyrians. They loved war. Assyrian soldiers were fierce and cruel, with strong armour and swift chariots. They conquered one land after another.

Soon they came to the Promised Land. Now it was the turn of Jerusalem to be surrounded by Assyrian soldiers. Their general shouted to the terrified people on the city walls. 'Why don't you be sensible and surrender? Your king can't save you! Nor will your God! Gods haven't saved any other cities!'

The king sent for Isaiah, the man of God. 'What shall I do?' he said anxiously.

'Have no fear,' said Isaiah. 'The Assyrians will go back to their own land. That is God's promise to you.'

The king trusted Isaiah, and refused to give in. Then came a letter from the Emperor of Assyria himself. 'Give in at once,' he ordered, 'or it will be all the worse for you.' The king took the letter into the temple, and prayed to God to save Jerusalem.

A message came from Isaiah: 'God has heard your prayer. He will not let Jerusalem fall to the proud Assyrians.'

Then, suddenly, the Assyrian soldiers were struck by plague so they broke up their camp and hurried away. Jerusalem had been saved from giving in by the faith of Isaiah, the man of God.

A discovery in the temple

Young King Josiah loved God dearly. He was eager to bring the chosen people back to the God of their fathers. The last king had made the people worship the evil gods of the Assyrians. Even the temple of God at Jerusalem had been left to fall into ruins.

Josiah ordered the people to collect money to repair the temple. The money was to buy fine wood and good stone and to pay the workmen. Soon the temple was swarming with carpenters, stone-masons and builders. The king ordered his secretary to look after the work.

One morning the king's secretary came to him with strange news. 'The high priest found this scroll among the rubbish in the temple,' he said.

'Read it to me,' said the king. How excited Josiah was when he heard what was written on the scroll. It was a new law for the people of God. It told how they should love God and how they should love each other.

Then King Josiah gathered all the people together at the temple. There they made their solemn promise to God to live by his new law – the law of love for God and for neighbours.

Jeremiah in prison

Jerusalem had been captured by the soldiers of Babylon. But the people rebelled, so again the army of Babylon surrounded the city. Jeremiah, the man of God, gave no hope to the people. 'Jerusalem will be taken,' he said. The leaders of the city hated him for this.

One day Jeremiah went to visit his home near the city.

'You're deserting to the enemy!' cried the guard at the city gate. He seized Jeremiah and the leaders of the city threw him into prison.

'He's a traitor!' they said to the king. 'He deserves to die!'

'Do what you will with him,' said the cowardly king.

They were afraid to kill a man of God. They lowered him into an old water pit, cut in the rock. It was deep in mud and slime. They left Jeremiah there to die.

An old slave in the palace went to the king. 'They have left the man of God in the pit. He will die there and bring God's anger upon us. Let me save him.'

The king gave him permission, and the slave hurried to the pit with his men. They dropped old rags down to Jeremiah to put under his arms, and ropes to tie over them. Then they slowly dragged Jeremiah up out of the thick mud in the stinking pit.

So Jeremiah was saved from death to go on bravely speaking for God.

Strangers in Babylon

Jerusalem had been captured by the soldiers of Babylon and its walls broken down. The people of God had been taken away from the Promised Land to live in Babylon. They had lost everything – their land, their holy city, their temple of God. Now they were strangers in a strange land.

They made a sad song, telling how miserable they were: 'We sat down by the waters of Babylon, and we wept when we remembered Jerusalem. We hung our harps on the willow trees. The people of Babylon said, "Take down your harps and sing us one of your merry songs." But how could we make music to God in a strange land?'

Babylon was a wonderful city, with fine streets, and beautiful buildings. Many were temples of the gods of Babylon. There were statues and idols of these gods everywhere. Often the strangers watched glorious processions through the streets in honour of the gods. The strangers began to worry. Were these gods greater than their God? Had they left God behind in Jerusalem? Had he forsaken his chosen people?

'No!' cried a great man of God. 'There is only one God! He is Lord of the whole earth! He is everywhere! He will lead you back to his holy city of Jerusalem!'

The one God of all

The people of Babylon were worried, for their empire was in danger. Cyrus, a ruler of the Persian people, had conquered many lands. Now his armies were coming close to Babylon.

But there was new hope for the people of God who had been taken to Babylon and made to live there. It came from a great man of God.

'Rejoice! Rejoice, my people!' was his message from God. 'God has raised up Cyrus to conquer Babylon, and to set you free! For God is Lord of all nations. He rules over earth and heaven.

'Have no fear of the gods of Babylon. How foolish these people are! Rich men get idols shaped from metal, and covered with gold – and then bow down before them! Poor men chop down a tree, use some of it for firewood, shape the rest into an idol, paint it over – and then kneel down before it! They worship lumps of wood and bits of metal – and call them gods!

'The one God of all dwells high in the heavens, in all his glory. But he is close to his people too. He cares for you tenderly, like a shepherd caring for his sheep. He will lead you back to the Promised Land, and to his holy city of Jerusalem.'

77

Nehemiah rebuilds Jerusalem

Nehemiah, one of the people of God, was cup-bearer to the great Emperor of Persia, and was always with him.

One day the emperor said: 'Why do you look so sad?'

Then Nehemiah told him the bad news from Jerusalem. 'My people tried to rebuild the city walls. But the governor stopped them. No one can live in the city, for enemies often attack it.'

'What would you like me to do?' said the emperor.

'My lord, give me leave to go and rebuild the city of my fathers.' Then the emperor gave him letters ordering his governors to help Nehemiah.

So Nehemiah came to Jerusalem. He told no one who he was. He spent all day going through the city. All night he and his servants rode on asses round the ruins of the walls. Next morning he called the leaders of the people together. He showed them the royal letters. 'God has sent me to rebuild the walls,' he said. 'I have examined them thoroughly. Each family will build one part. Here are your orders.'

The work was hard. Half the men had to stand on guard, in case of attack. But Nehemiah drove the people on until the walls were finished.

Then Jerusalem was strong and safe, and people could live there again. Nehemiah could go back to the emperor, knowing that he had done his work for God.

The story of Ruth

In the town of Bethlehem there once lived a lady named
Naomi, with her husband and their two sons. When famine
came to the Promised Land they went to live in the land of
Moab, where there was plenty of food. When Naomi's sons
grew up they married ladies of Moab, named Ruth and
Orpah.

One day Naomi's husband and her two sons fell ill and
died. Naomi had to go back to her own land, where her
people would look after her. Ruth and Orpah had to stay with
their own people. But when Naomi said goodbye to them
Ruth would not leave her.

'Don't send me away,' Ruth pleaded. 'Where you go I will go. Where you live I will live. Your people shall be my people. Your God shall be my God.'

So Naomi and Ruth came to Bethlehem. It was harvest time, and Ruth soon found work in the field of good Farmer Boaz. He admired Ruth for coming to a strange land, and worshipping a strange God. Soon he married Ruth, and now she belonged to the people of God. A son was born to them, and from his family came the great King David.

Some of the people of God thought that God did not care about strangers and foreigners. But, said this story, David himself came from a foreign lady! So God loves all people.

81

The story of Jonah

There once lived a man of God named Jonah. One night God called him: 'Go to the people of Nineveh, and turn them from their evil ways.'

Jonah was horrified. 'What!' he cried. 'Go to those wicked Assyrians, with their evil gods, and their terrible soldiers? No I won't! I'll flee away and hide from God.'

Jonah took a ship sailing far away. A fierce storm blew up, and the sailors were terrified. Then Jonah told them that he was fleeing from his God, and must have made him angry.

'Throw me into the sea!' cried Jonah. 'It's all my fault!' So the sailors threw him overboard, and Jonah was swallowed by

a great whale. Then, after three days and nights, the whale spewed him out on to dry land.

Again God called Jonah to go to Nineveh. This time he went. The people of Nineveh were sorry for their evil ways, and turned to God. Jonah was horrified that God forgave them all their wicked deeds.

Jonah sat under a tree feeling miserable. Next day the tree had withered and died, and Jonah felt sorry for it.

Then God said to him: 'Jonah, you feel sorry for that tree. Won't you let me feel sorry for all the men and women and children of Nineveh?'

Some of the chosen people were like Jonah. They thought that God did not care for people of other lands. But this story said that God cares for all people.

The story of Daniel

Daniel was a boy when the people of God were taken away to the land of Babylon. There he grew into a good and wise man. The King of Babylon made him a ruler of his kingdom. But the princes and nobles of Babylon were jealous of Daniel. They tricked the king into making a new law. It said that only the king could give blessings. A man who asked a blessing from anyone else must be thrown to the lions.

They easily caught Daniel. Three times a day he opened his window facing towards Jerusalem, knelt down, and prayed to God for a blessing.

'We caught him asking a blessing from his God,' they said to the king. The king was angry with himself for letting them trick him. He tried hard to save Daniel. But he could not break his own law. So Daniel was cast into the den of lions.

The king went sadly to his palace for the night. He could not eat, or drink, or sleep. As soon as it was light he hurried to the lions' den. 'Daniel!' he cried, dreading that there would be no answer.

But Daniel answered him, 'Fear not, O King! My God has guarded me, for he knows that I have done you no wrong.'

Then the happy king ordered his men to bring Daniel out. He honoured the God of Daniel who had saved him. Daniel had been true to God, and refused to worship idols. The people of God must be like him.

Judas the Hammerer

The Promised Land was ruled over by a Greek king. He believed in the Greek gods, and ordered the people of God to worship his idols. He sent his soldiers to capture Jerusalem and make the people obey him. His huge army had lots of armour, and elephants too. But it could only fight on flat land.

Judas was a fine warrior. He and his men lived in the hills. They swooped down to attack the Greek soldiers, and hit them hard – just like a hammer. Then they disappeared back into the hills. So Judas was called the Hammerer of the Greek army. Judas won great victories over the Greek soldiers, and at last he drove them from Jerusalem.

Judas and his men wept when they saw the temple of God in ruins. For three years it had been filled with Greek idols. Judas and his men threw them out, and repaired the temple.

A great festival was held to bless the temple again as the house of God. It was lit up with lamps and candles, and shone again in all its glory.

The coming of the Romans

Judas the Hammerer heard of a great people called the Romans. They had given law and peace to the lands they had conquered. Judas sent two trusted men to Rome, and they made friends with the Romans.

But soon afterwards Judas was killed in battle. Then there were other leaders. They often quarrelled and fought against each other. It was like this when a Roman general named

Pompey was in a country nearby. He decided to end the fighting, and he marched his army to Jerusalem. Pompey laid seige to the holy city and captured it.

General Pompey wanted to find out more about the people of God. He marched into the temple to see what their God was like. He even strode into the holy of holies, the most sacred part of their temple. He expected to see a great idol. But it was quite empty. Their God was not made of wood or stone.

The Promised Land was made part of the great Roman Empire. The Romans chose a clever ruler named Herod the Great to rule over the people of God. And Herod was their king when a very special baby was born in the little town of Bethlehem. His name was Jesus.

Baby Jesus

The little town of Bethlehem was crowded with people. They had come to be counted, as the Romans had ordered. Joseph was troubled as he led his ass into Bethlehem. Mary, sitting on the ass, was tired after their long journey. The time was near for her baby to be born. Joseph was anxious to find a resting-place for her.

'No room at the inn,' said the inn-keeper. 'You can go in the stable if you like – plenty of clean straw there.' So Joseph made a bed for Mary in the stable, with oxen and asses standing by. There Mary gave birth to her first-born son. An angel had told her, long before, that he should be called Jesus.

Baby Jesus was washed, and folded in a cloth. Then strips of linen were wrapped round him, like bandages. This swaddling would help his limbs to grow straight. Jesus was laid in one of the stone mangers. There he was safe and cosy and warm, in his bed of clean straw.

'Jesus' means 'God saves'. Baby Jesus had been sent by God to save his people. So Jesus the Saviour was born, not in a royal palace, but in a stable at Bethlehem.

Shepherds visit Jesus

It was a cold night when Jesus was born in a stable at Bethlehem. Out on the hills the shepherds wrapped their cloaks around them. Their sheep were safe inside the high stone walls of the fold.

Above the shepherds the dark blue sky sparkled with twinkling stars. Suddenly a dazzling light filled the sky like the glory of God. The terrified shepherds heard a voice: 'Fear not! I bring you news of great joy! This day in Bethlehem the Saviour is born! You will find him there, lying in a manger!' Then came the swelling sound of heavenly music. The dazzling light seemed like a great choir of angels singing the praises of God.

The music died away, the light faded, and the shepherds were alone. They turned to each other in amazement. What could it mean? 'Let's go to Bethlehem and see!' they all cried.

So they left their sheep safe in the fold and hurried down the hillside. They came to the inn and saw the glimmer of light from the stable. They tiptoed inside. They saw Joseph, and Mary, and the baby in the manger – just as the voice had said. They sank to their knees, full of wonder at the strange happenings of that night.

Wise men visit Jesus

Far away in the east there were wise men who studied the stars. They believed that the stars ruled over the world. They were looking for a Saviour to come from heaven, just like the people of God.

One night they saw a brilliant new star. It told them that the Saviour had been born. The star would lead them to him. Three wise men set off to follow the star. They rode on their camels, and took precious gifts with them. The star led them to the holy city of Jerusalem.

Old King Herod was cruel and trusted no one. When he heard of strangers seeking a newborn king he sent for them.

'Come back and tell me where you've found him,' Herod said.
'Then I'll go and worship him too.'

The star led them to Bethlehem, and there they knelt before
Jesus. They laid their costly presents before him. The first
wise man gave him gold – used by kings. The second gave him
incense – used for the worship of God. The third gave him
myrrh – a fragrant oil used when burying the dead.

The wise men set off home by another road. For they had
been warned in a dream not to tell Herod about the newborn
king. They took back with them the wonderful tidings that a
Saviour from heaven had been born into the world.

The boy Jesus at Nazareth

Jesus grew up in a small town called Nazareth. His home was a little white-washed house. The staircase was outside, and it led up to the cool, flat roof where the children played. Jesus watched his mother Mary at work, sweeping the floor, baking bread, making clothes. He went with her to the well each day to fetch water.

Mary had taught Jesus about his heavenly father. Jesus went to school with his friends. There they learnt to read and to write and to count. Their books were the holy writings of their Bible.

When school was over the children dashed out to play. They made slings for hurling pebbles at a target. They cut pipes and whistles from reeds to make music. They played games with pebbles, too.

Jesus saw God at work in nature. He loved flowers and birds and animals. He went with the shepherds on the hills. He went to the farms of his friends. He went with the fishermen on the Sea of Galilee. In the market-place he saw all kinds of people, buying and selling, gossiping and arguing.

Mary was married to a carpenter named Joseph. Jesus learnt from Joseph how to make things from wood. He would be able to earn his living as a wood-worker when he grew up.

The boy Jesus at Jerusalem

One day Jesus woke up very excited. He was going on his first journey. For he was twelve years old, and he was going to Jerusalem to visit the temple of God. His friends were going, too.

Each family had its donkey, loaded with things for camping at night. Jesus was with his friends most of the time. But Mary did not worry, for she knew that he was safe.

How excited Jesus was to see Jerusalem, and to come to the beautiful temple of God. He loved spending most of the time talking to the teachers in the temple.

Soon they began the journey back home. Mary thought that Jesus was with his friends. But when night came she could not find Jesus in any of the tents. Early next morning she hurried back to Jerusalem with Joseph. For three days they searched. Then they went to the temple – and there was Jesus with the teachers.

'How could you treat us like this!' Mary cried, her worry turning to anger. 'We've been searching everywhere! Didn't you realise we'd be worried?'

Jesus was surprised. 'Why did you search for me, mother? Didn't you realise I'd be in my father's house?'

Jesus went back to Nazareth with them. He was a good son, working in the carpenter's shop. But Mary knew that Jesus had much more important work to do for his heavenly father, when the time came.

John the Baptist

Jesus had a cousin named John. When John grew up he knew that he had work to do for God. He went out to live in the lonely desert. He wore a rough camel-skin. He ate wild honey and insects. He was alone, except for lizards and scorpions and snakes.

Each day John went to a ford where people had to wade across the River Jordan. It was a fine place to meet travellers and to speak to them of God. The news spread far and wide – God had sent a new messenger to his people.

John was a wild man, with his rough dress, fiery hair, flashing eyes and thundering voice. His words were stern and

fierce and frightening. He told people that God was angry with their evil ways and would punish them. Their only hope was to be sorry, to come down into the water, and to have their evil washed away by his baptizing.

People kept asking John who he was. John said: 'I am a messenger, a herald. You know how a slave runs before a royal procession shouting, "Clear the road! Make way for the king!" That is what I am. I am preparing the way for one who comes after me. I'm not even worthy to kneel before him and untie his sandals.'

'Who does he mean?' everyone was asking.

100

Jesus is baptized

Some people said that John was a madman. But others heard him gladly and their hearts were stirred. John went down into the waters of the River Jordan with them and baptized them. Then they could begin a new life. One day when John had finished he was amazed to see his cousin Jesus standing before him.

'Why do you come to me?' he said to Jesus humbly. 'I am the one who needs to be washed and born again – not you. You should baptize me.'

But Jesus answered: 'It is the will of God.'

So Jesus was baptized by John. Jesus felt the Spirit of God coming upon him, like a dove gently settling on his shoulder. He heard the voice of his heavenly father saying: 'This is my beloved son.'

John was glad that Jesus had come to him. For it showed that John was indeed his herald. He had prepared the way. Now the king himself had come.

One day, much later, the sad news came to Jesus that John had been cruelly put to death by the evil King Herod. Jesus said to the people: 'There has never lived a greater man than John. For he was the herald, preparing the way for the Kingdom of God.'

Jesus is tempted

After Jesus had been baptized by John he went out into the
desert to be alone. He had always known that he was the
Saviour, sent by God to his people. He had to decide – what
kind of Saviour would he be? How would he bring men to
love God?

Messengers of God had often promised that God would
send a Saviour to set up his kingdom on earth. What would
the kingdom of God be like? People thought that the
Saviour would bring them riches, instead of them being
poor and hungry. He would show them great wonders and
marvels. He would drive out the Romans and give them a fine
kingdom of their own.

How popular Jesus would be if he was that kind of Saviour!
Out in the desert he was tempted to be like that. But he knew
it was all wrong. God loves people, and he wants them to love
him. Then his kingdom of peace and goodness and love grows
in their hearts. It does not come from having worldly riches,
or seeing great wonders, or fighting battles.

So Jesus decided what kind of Saviour he would be. He
would show men the love of God in his words, in his deeds, in
his life, even in his death. He was sure and strong. He could
begin his work for his heavenly father.

Jesus at Nazareth

When Jesus came back from the desert he went first to
Nazareth. It was his home-town where he had grown up and
worked as a carpenter.

It was the Sabbath Day, the holy day of the week. Jesus
went to the service at the synagogue, the church where he had

been to school and worshipped God. During the service Jesus was invited to read a lesson from the Bible and to speak about it. He chose a reading which told of the coming of God's kingdom. Then he said: 'Today these words have come true. God has sent me to proclaim the Good News that his kingdom has come.'

At first the people listened to the fine words of Jesus. Then they began to whisper to each other. 'Isn't this man Jesus the carpenter?' they muttered. 'Who does he think he is? Why, he used to make and mend our tools!' They grew angry and spoke louder.

'No man of God is welcomed by his own people,' Jesus said, above the hubbub.

They could stand no more. They crowded round Jesus as he walked out, shouting and shaking their fists at him. They followed him to the hill he knew so well, until he disappeared into the caves.

Jesus never went back to Nazareth again. He went to other towns and villages, telling the Good News that God's kingdom had come on earth.

Jesus calls fishermen

Jesus needed men to help him in his work. What kind of people would he choose?

One day Jesus walked by the Sea of Galilee, famous for its fish. He had many friends among the fishermen. Each group worked together with their own boat and nets.

Jesus called out to the brothers Andrew and Simon. They were out in their boat, casting their nets. When they heard Jesus they soon came to shore.

'Come! Follow me,' said Jesus. 'You are fishermen. I will make you fishers of men.' The brothers knew Jesus and believed in him. They gladly followed him.

Further on Jesus came to the brothers James and John. They were mending their nets.

'James! John!' Jesus called. 'Come, follow me.' They, too, gladly followed the man they had come to love.

Jesus knew the men he had chosen. They were strong, and honest, and true. He gave Simon a new name. It was Peter which means rock. He gave a fine nickname to James and John who were fiery young men. He called them sons of thunder.

They had been gathering fish into their nets. Instead, they would gather people into the kingdom of God. They were always with Jesus, helping him in his work.

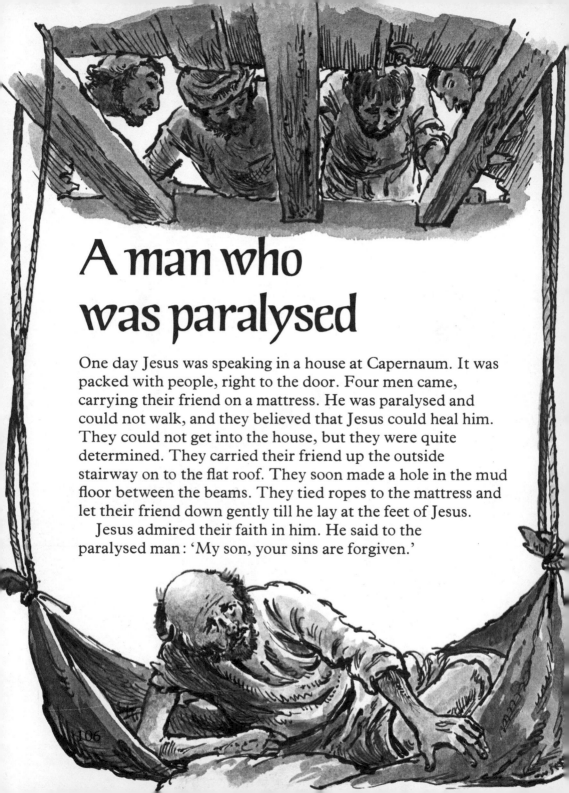

A man who was paralysed

One day Jesus was speaking in a house at Capernaum. It was packed with people, right to the door. Four men came, carrying their friend on a mattress. He was paralysed and could not walk, and they believed that Jesus could heal him. They could not get into the house, but they were quite determined. They carried their friend up the outside stairway on to the flat roof. They soon made a hole in the mud floor between the beams. They tied ropes to the mattress and let their friend down gently till he lay at the feet of Jesus.

Jesus admired their faith in him. He said to the paralysed man: 'My son, your sins are forgiven.'

Some of the people in the crowd were horrified. 'Who does this man think he is?' they said angrily to each other. 'Only God can forgive sins!'

Jesus knew what they were thinking. 'Which is easier?' he said to them. 'To say to this paralysed man, "Your sins are forgiven," or to say, "Get up and walk"? You must know that I have power to forgive sins.' Then Jesus said to the man: 'Stand up, pick up your mattress and go home.'

The man got up, rolled up his mattress, and walked out of the house.

'We never saw anything like this!' everybody said.

Jesus calls a tax-collector

Matthew Levi lived in the town of Capernaum by the Sea of Galilee. It was a busy port for fishermen. Many travellers came there too, for the great Roman road ran through Capernaum. Fishermen and travellers had to pay taxes to the Romans at the customs-house there. Matthew Levi was the tax-collector.

People hated the Romans who had conquered their land. So they hated even more the men who collected taxes for the Romans, because they were traitors to their people. Matthew Levi was rich in money – he had lots. He was poor in friends – he had very few.

One day Matthew Levi sat at his table counting the money.

A shadow fell over his table and a voice said: 'Come, Matthew. Follow me.' He looked up. It was Jesus, the man everyone was talking about. Jesus wanted him! He was so excited that he jumped up at once and followed Jesus.

That night Matthew Levi gave a party at his house for his friends to meet Jesus. They were hated men, too.

Good people were horrified. 'How can you sit and feast with such evil men?' they said to Jesus.

'Only sick people need a doctor,' Jesus answered. 'You are sure of your goodness – you don't need God's love. I have come to call people who need the love and mercy of God.'

109

Jesus the friend of children

Jesus showed God's love to everyone. He was a friend to all – but especially to children. One day he called a little boy named David, sat him on his knees, and put his arms round him. Jesus knew that his helpers were beginning to think too much of themselves. 'You must be like this child,' he said, 'if you want to enter the kingdom of God.'

David never forgot that kind man. One day he and his sister Miriam went to play in the market-place. They met their friends, and soon they were all playing at weddings and funerals. For a wedding the boys danced, stamping feet and clapping hands, and the girls set the time with their hand-drums and rattles. For a funeral the girls wailed out loud, with groans and shrieks, and the boys played shrill, sad music on their pipes and flutes.

Suddenly David saw the kind man coming into the market-place with his helpers. He dashed home to tell his mother and her friends. The mothers hurried back with him and tried to get close to Jesus with their children.

'Don't bother Jesus now,' said his fussy helpers. 'He's busy talking.' The mothers turned away sadly.

Then the voice of Jesus rang out angrily: 'Let the children come to me!' So the people made way, and the mothers brought their children to Jesus to be blessed one by one.

The daughter of Jairus

One day Jesus sat in Peter's boat, just off the beach, so that everyone could hear him. Suddenly there was a stir in the crowd. A man named Jairus was trying to get to Jesus. When he reached the boat he fell on his knees weeping.

'Master,' he sobbed, 'it's my little daughter Rachel. I'm afraid she's dying. If only you will come I know you can save her. She's only twelve years old,' he wept.

'I will come at once,' said Jesus.

As they made their way up the crowded street a servant of Jairus hurried towards them. 'Rachel is dead, sir,' he said. 'Why bother Jesus any more?'

'Just trust in me,' Jesus said to Jairus.

112

The house was crowded with mourners. Some were wailing aloud, others were playing shrill music on flutes.

'Why make all this noise?' Jesus said. 'The child is not dead but sleeping.' The mourners mocked him.

Jesus bade Jairus send them out of the house. Then he went in to the little girl. Rachel lay still on her bed. Jesus took her hand. 'Little girl, it's time to wake up,' he said gently. Rachel stirred and sighed and opened her eyes. Then she sat up and smiled.

'Give her something to eat,' Jesus said to her parents. 'Make sure you tell no one what has happened.'

The son of Chuza

Chuza and his wife Joanna lived in a fine house at Capernaum.
For Chuza was the steward of King Herod, and looked after
his royal court. One day their little son Philip was very ill with
a fever. The royal doctor could do nothing, and Philip grew
worse. Then Joanna told Chuza how Jesus healed the sick,
and he galloped furiously to the town of Cana where Jesus
was staying.

People stared at Chuza's fine horse and his royal uniform as
he hurried to the house where Jesus was speaking.

'Were you looking for me?' Jesus said kindly.

'Please, please help me,' Chuza said anxiously. 'It's my son.
He's very ill with a fever.'

'People won't believe in me unless I do wonders,' Jesus said
sadly. 'I expect you are like that too.'

'Please, master!', Chuza said desperately. 'Please come now
before he dies!'

Then Jesus saw Chuza's great faith and said to him: 'Go in
peace. Your son will live.'

Chuza hurried home. Servants ran out to greet him.
'Philip's better!' they shouted joyfully.

'When did the fever leave him?' Chuza asked. And then he
knew that it was at the very moment when Jesus had spoken.

'How can we thank Jesus?' Chuza said to his wife.

'Only by following him,' she replied. So Joanna became a
disciple of Jesus.

114

The mustard seed

The mustard plant was very common in the land of Jesus, for it grew wild. It was famous for its seed which was the smallest of all seeds. People made a saying from it. If something was very tiny they said it was 'like a mustard seed'. But the mustard was famous for something else, too. It soon grew into a plant, with bright yellow flowers. Then it became a thick bush. Then it grew as big as a tree, with branches spreading far and wide, so that birds perched on its branches and found shelter in it. From the tiniest seed came a great tree.

The helpers of Jesus were troubled. Lots of people came to Jesus. They came just to see him, or to listen to his fine stories, or to be healed by him. But not many became followers of Jesus. How could the kingdom of God grow from such tiny beginnings?

'It is like the mustard seed,' Jesus said to them. 'We are sowing the seed of God's kingdom in the hearts of men. At first it is very small, just like the mustard. But it will grow, like the mustard seed, into a mighty tree. Just as birds find shelter in the mustard tree so men will find shelter in the kingdom of God.'

The lost sheep

Benjamin was proud of looking after his father's flock of a hundred sheep. Every morning he led them to good pasture. Every evening he led them to the stone fold, counted them as they went in, and guarded them through the night.

One evening his counting showed that one was missing. He left the flock safe in the fold with the other shepherds and ran all the way home. 'Father! Father!' he shouted, banging on the door. 'One of the lambs is missing!'

Soon Benjamin and his father were hurrying through the darkness – there were so many dangers for sheep. At last they heard a frightened bleating. Their lamb had fallen over a cliff and was trapped in a bush. Benjamin lifted the lamb gently with his crook, held it close inside his cloak, and they set off home.

Benjamin's father was so happy that he called all their neighbours in for a party. 'We've found our lamb!' he cried. 'Come and share our joy!'

Benjamin thought to himself: 'I want to be a good shepherd like father. He's happier over finding one lost sheep than over all the other sheep safe in the fold.'

This story of Jesus' explains what God is like. He loves each of his children. God is happier over one person who comes back to him than over all the good people already safe in his care.

The lost coin

Miriam was proud of the circle of small coins that she wore round her forehead, over her head-dress. They had been given to her on her wedding-day. They were her treasure, too. So she was horrified when, one morning, she found that a coin had dropped off. She must search for her lost coin till she found it.

The house was one large room, and the floor was simply the earth. It was dark too, with only one small window high up. Miriam lit the oil-lamp, took her broom of palm leaves, and began to sweep. She swept all over the floor but found nothing. Then she went down on hands and knees, with the lamp beside her, and went over the floor again, bit by bit. She searched all morning. Then she saw something shiny in the dust. At last! She had found her lost coin.

How happy Miriam was! She rushed into the street and shouted to her neighbours: 'I've found my lost coin! Come and share my joy!'

What a good time they had! As the neighbours said, Miriam was happier over finding one lost coin then over all the other coins safely on her forehead.

It is just like that with God, Jesus was saying. He is happier over finding one lost person than over all the good people who are safely with him.

The lost son

Farmer Boaz was a happy man. He had a fine farm, and two sons whom he loved dearly. His money would be shared between them by law. Simon, his elder son, was content to work on the land. But Jason, his younger son, grew bored with the dull life on the farm.

One day he went to his father and said: 'Father, give me my share of your money now. I want to travel and make my fortune.' Farmer Boaz agreed, but how sad he was to see his dear son leave.

Jason went to a foreign city. He had a wonderful time. With lots of money he had lots of friends. But soon his father's money was all gone – and so were his friends. Now he was alone and poor in a strange land. He could not get work anywhere. At last a farmer said Jason could look after his pigs. He was so hungry that he ate the pigs' rough food.

Jason began to think, 'Here I am, a hungry beggar. At home even the servants are better off. I'll go back home. I'll tell my father how bad I've been. I'll say: "I'm not fit to be called your son. Please give me a job on your farm!"'

Farmer Boaz ran to welcome the ragged beggar. Jason

found it hard to say his words as his father hugged him and called servants. 'Bring fine clothes! Prepare a rich feast! For my son was lost – and now he's found!'

The lost son and his brother

As Simon trudged back from a hard day on the farm he heard music and singing and dancing. He called a servant. 'What's all the noise about?' he demanded.

'Your brother's come back home, and your father's made a feast for him,' the servant said.

Simon was furious. 'What!' shouted Simon to the servant. 'A feast just because that good-for-nothing has come back? I'm not going in! And you can go and tell my father!'

Farmer Boaz hurried out to plead with Simon.

But Simon shouted rudely at him too. 'All these years I've slaved on your farm! You never gave a party for me! But what happens when that lazy son of yours comes back – after throwing your money away on the layabouts of the city? Why, he gets a grand feast!'

Jason's heart was greedy and selfish. Simon's heart was hard and bitter. Most fathers would have felt like Simon and turned Jason out. But the love in the heart of Farmer Boaz was like the love of God for all his children.

'Simon my dear son,' he said gently, 'you are always with me. But Jason is my son too, and I love you both dearly. I was afraid that I would never see him again. How could I not rejoice when he came back home? He was lost – and now he's found. Come in to the feast and share my joy. Then my happiness will be complete.'

A woman in the crowd

There was always a crowd of people around Jesus. Some wanted to see him. Some wanted to hear his teaching. Some wanted to be healed by him.

One day there was a woman in the crowd who was determined to get close to Jesus. She had been ill for many years, and no doctor had been able to heal her. When she heard of Jesus and his healing power she believed in him. 'I know he can heal me,' she said to herself. 'I'll get close to him. If I just take hold of a tassel on his cloak I'll be healed.'

At last she stood right behind Jesus. She bent down and gently took one of the tassels in her hand. At once she knew that she was better.

But Jesus knew that power had gone out of him. He turned round: 'Who touched my cloak?' he asked.

The disciples were astonished. 'Why do you ask who touched you when there is such a crowd jostling around you?'

The woman fell on her knees, trembling with fear, and told Jesus everything.

'Your faith has saved you,' Jesus said to the woman gently. 'Be healed, and go in peace.'

The good neighbour

Jacob had finished his business at Jerusalem. He hurried home to Jericho along the lonely and dangerous road through the wild hills. Robbers attacked him, took his money, and left him lying badly wounded in the blazing sun.

A priest came along the road, hurrying to the temple in Jerusalem. He took one look at Jacob and quickly passed by on the other side of the road. Later came a Levite, a servant of the priests at the temple. He too hurried past on the other side of the road.

Later on came a Samaritan. He was an enemy of the people of God. But when he saw Jacob he got off his donkey at once and bound up his wounds. He lifted Jacob on to the donkey,

and took him to the inn where he hired a room for Jacob. Next
morning before leaving he gave two silver coins to the
innkeeper. 'Take good care of my friend,' he said. 'If you
spend more than that I'll repay you on my way back.'

Jesus had said that there are two great commandments –
love God, and love your neighbour as yourself.

A young man had asked him: 'Who is my neighbour?'

Jesus told him this story. Then he said: 'Which of those
three men was a good neighbour to Jacob?'

'The one who was kind to him,' the man replied.

'Then you go and be a good neighbour like him,' said
Jesus to the young man.

The light of the world

In the land of Jesus, a house was one big room. There was no glass. A big window would let in sun and wind and rain – and thieves too. So there was only one small window high up in the wall. The house was so dark that the lamp was kept burning all night, and most of the day too. It was made of clay. It had a handle for carrying. There was one hole for the wick, made of flax, and another hole for pouring in the olive oil.

Jesus said to his followers: 'When you light the lamp you don't put it under a bed, or under a basin, do you? Of course not. You put it on a lamp-stand so that it lights up the whole house. You are to be like the lamp. Let your light shine out so that everyone can see it. They will see the love and the goodness of God shining brightly in everything you do. Then they will know that your light comes from God. And they will give glory to him.'

But how did the followers of Jesus come to know the light of God's goodness and love? They saw it shining perfectly in Jesus. So they knew exactly what Jesus meant when he said: 'I am the light of the world.'

Finding treasure

In the time of Jesus, people hid their money in the ground. 'The safest place for money is the earth,' they said. For only the man who had secretly buried it knew where it was. But he might suddenly die, or go on a journey and never return. Then his money lay in the earth and no one knew. The law said that if someone found a buried treasure like this on his land he could keep it.

One day a man was walking across an old field. He stumbled against something hard in the ground. He was curious, and he got down and scraped away the earth. How delighted he was to find a strong box full of buried treasure. He quickly covered it up, and hurried into the town to buy that field. He had to sell everything he owned to buy it – his house, his clothes, his ox, his ass, his goat. Then he had enough money to buy that field and the treasure was his.

Jesus said that the kingdom of God is like that. A man may come across it quite by chance. But when he has found it he knows that it is the greatest treasure of all. He gives up everything to win it. Then he has his treasure in heaven.

Seeking pearls

There was once a merchant who traded in pearls. He did not buy and sell them just to make money. He did it because he loved pearls more than anything in the world. He travelled far and wide, always searching for finer and more beautiful pearls. One day, on his travels, he found the loveliest pearl he had ever seen. It was a perfect pearl. 'I must have it,' he said to himself. 'I can't live without it.' The owner promised to keep it for him, and he hurried back home to raise the money to buy it.

The price of that perfect pearl was enormous. The merchant was quite rich, but even he had to sell everything he owned to raise the money – his fine house, his fields and his animals, and all his own beloved pearls. But to have that beautiful pearl was worth giving up everything.

People like this merchant do not find the kingdom of God by chance, like a man stumbling across buried treasure. They have to search hard and long before they find it. But when they have found it they know that it is worth far more than all they possess. It is the finest treasure of all.

Using our talents

A certain rich man was going on a journey. He called three of his servants. 'I'm going to trust you with my money while I'm away,' he said. 'Use it well, and make as much money as you can for me.' He gave five bags of gold, called talents, to Jacob his best servant; two bags to Benjamin, the next best; and one bag to Reuben who was not so able.

Jacob traded cleverly in costly silks and spices, and he doubled his money. Benjamin traded in salt fish and dried fruits, and he too doubled his money. Reuben hid his bag of gold safely in the ground.

When their master got back he sent for them.

'I've doubled your money, master!' said Jacob, proudly putting ten bags of gold on the table.

'Well done!' said his master. 'I'll make you my steward!'

Benjamin put six bags on the table. 'I've doubled your money too, master!' he said.

'Well done, Benjamin. I'll make you my second steward.'

Then Reuben dumped his bag on the table. 'I was afraid of losing your money so I hid it safely in the ground,' he said.

'You lazy rascal! From you I gain nothing,' cried his master. 'Throw him out of my house!' he ordered.

God trusts everyone with gifts we call talents. We must use them in his service if we are to be true and faithful servants.

131

A blind man

One day Jesus came to the little town of Bethsaida. A man was led to Jesus by his friends. He was almost blind. He could just make out the shape of trees so as not to walk into them. But that was all.

'Please lay your hands on him, master,' said his friends, pleading with Jesus.

Jesus took the man by the hand, and led him out of the town, away from the crowd. When they were alone he anointed the man's eyes and laid his hands on them. 'Can you see anything?' Jesus asked.

'Why, yes!' said the man, getting excited. 'I can see trees walking about! They must be people!' Then Jesus again laid his hands on the man's eyes.

'Now I can see clearly!' cried the man joyfully. 'I can see everything!'

Jesus said to him: 'Go back home quietly. Don't go into the town. And don't tell anyone what God has done for you.'

132

The birds of the air

Jesus lived in Galilee, a land of streams and gentle hills. On the hill-sides were trees and shrubs, orchards of olives and pomegranates, and fruitful vineyards. So it was the home of many different kinds of birds.

Jesus saw God at work in the ways of nature and he often spoke about them to the people. 'Why do you worry so much?' he said. 'You're always thinking about food, and drink, and clothes. Look up at the flock of birds wheeling in

the sky. They don't worry. Birds don't sow seeds, and reap corn, and carefully store the harvest in barns. Yet your father in heaven provides food for them. And you are much more precious to him than they are.

'Listen to the twittering of the sparrows in that olive-tree. They're common enough, aren't they? You know how cheap they are in the market-place. But God cares for them. Not a single sparrow is forgotten by him. And you are much more valuable to him than a whole flock of sparrows.

'So don't worry. Don't be afraid. Put God first, and trust in him. He knows your needs. He will provide for you.'

The lilies of the field

Spring comes suddenly to the land of Galilee. All at once the bare brown hills and the rolling meadows are covered with a carpet of flowers, alive with beauty and colour. There are hosts of anemones, red and pink, purple and blue, cream and white. Mingling with them are many other flowers – lilies, irises, daisies and tulips. These were the 'lilies of the field' which Jesus saw as the handiwork of God.

'Why do you worry so much about clothes?' Jesus said to the people one spring. 'Just look at this carpet of flowers around us. They are wild flowers – they have not been planted by men. Nor do they work hard, labouring at weaving cloth to make clothes. Yet how beautiful they are! Even the great king Solomon, adorned in his royal robes, was never as glorious as these wild flowers. It is God who clothes them in all their beauty.

'But flowers which are alive today will be dead and thrown on the fire tomorrow. If God clothes them in such beauty for their brief life how much more will he clothe you – you who have so little trust in him. Set your heart on him and his goodness – not on clothes. He knows your needs. He will provide for you.'

137

Wise and foolish bridesmaids

In the land of Jesus, a wedding-feast was held in the evening at the bridegroom's house. His friends helped him to get ready. Then they went to the bride's house to fetch her and her bridesmaids, and they all made a happy procession to the wedding-feast. As it was dark they needed lights, and these were provided by the bridesmaids. Each of them carried a small clay lamp, with a wick burning in olive oil, to light up the procession.

Now it happened at a certain wedding that the bridegroom and his friends were very late and the bridesmaids' lamps were already flickering low. Five of them were wise girls. They had brought extra oil and they could soon refill their lamps and keep the lights burning.

'Give us some of your oil!' cried the five foolish girls who had not brought extra oil.

'We dare not,' said the wise girls, 'or we won't have enough for the procession. You must go and fetch oil for yourselves.'

The foolish girls hurried off. The happy procession went to the wedding-feast, and the door was shut and barred.

Then came loud banging and shouting: 'Please let us in! We're bridesmaids!'

The bridegroom called out: 'All my guests are here and the feast has started. I don't want strangers at my wedding-feast!'

Jesus invited people to enter into the kingdom of God. Some were careless about his invitation. They risked being shut out from the kingdom of God.

The friend at midnight

Levi lived a quiet life with his wife Mary, for they had no
children and few visitors. So how delighted he was when one
night his old friend Benjamin arrived, quite unexpectedly.
But how horrified he was when Mary told him she had no
bread left to give his friend supper. He must get some. His
friend Simeon would help him.

Simeon had a big family. They were all asleep, their
mattresses spread out over the platform on which the family
lived. Suddenly about midnight came a loud banging on the
door. Simeon awoke with a start.

Then came shouting: 'Simeon! It's your friend Levi! A
visitor has come and we've no bread! Lend me three loaves!
Please Simeon!'

Simeon was cross at being so rudely disturbed. 'Go away!'
he cried. 'The door is barred and my family asleep! I can't
disturb them all! Go away!'

But Levi was desperate. He had no shame. 'Three loaves!'

he yelled, banging away. 'Three loaves!'

Simeon got up angrily, clambered over the children, grabbed three loaves, opened the door, and threw the bread at Levi. Levi had got what he wanted by being persistent – by going on asking.

Be like Levi when you ask God for things in prayer, Jesus was saying. Be persistent. Go on asking. Your heavenly father will hear and answer your prayers.

A man with a disease

One day when Jesus was in the town of Capernaum a man came and knelt before him. He had a skin disease which made him ugly. There were strict rules for an illness like this. The priest decided how serious it was. If other people could catch it he ordered the man to live alone. But the man from Capernaum heard how Jesus healed the sick.

'This Jesus must be a wonder-worker,' the man said to himself. So he came to Jesus. 'Please heal me,' he said. 'I know you can, if you want to.'

Jesus was angry at the man's words. He was not a wonder-worker who healed people only if he wanted to. But he was sorry for the man. Jesus laid his hand on the man's head. 'I do wish to heal you,' he said. 'Now you are clean again.'

Then Jesus said to the man: 'Don't tell anyone about this. Go straight to the priest, as the law orders. Show him that you are healed and he will give you permission to go back home. Make your offerings, as the law orders, for being cured of your disease.'

But the man hurried off and spread the story of his wonderful healing all over the town. And the crowds flocked around Jesus more than ever.

The Pharisee and the tax-collector

Two men went to the temple of God to say their prayers. One of them was a Pharisee – a devout man who lived strictly by the sacred laws and never broke them. He was proud of himself and of his good deeds. He strode into the temple and stood where everyone could see him. He raised his hands and his eyes to heaven. It was the custom to say prayers out loud. 'God,' he said proudly, 'I thank you that I am not like other men. I am truthful and honest, I am just and fair and pure. I'm certainly nothing like that tax-collector over there!'

The tax-collector had crept into a corner where no one could see him. He knew that people hated and despised him as a traitor collecting taxes for the Romans. He was an outcast to both God and man. He stood with his head bowed, beating his breast with shame and sorrow. He could not hope for God's forgiveness – only for his mercy. 'God be merciful to me, sinner that I am,' he murmured.

The ending of this story shocked everyone.

'It was the tax-collector who was forgiven by God, not the Pharisee,' Jesus said. For there are no limits to God's love and

142

mercy. Those who trust in themselves are far from him. Those who trust only in his mercy are close to his heart.

The unforgiving governor

There was once a great emperor who ruled over many lands. He appointed a governor to rule over each land and to collect taxes for him. He found out that one governor had cheated him of a huge sum of money.

The emperor was furious. 'Sell him and his family as slaves,' he ordered. 'Sell all he owns to pay his debt!'

The proud governor threw himself at the emperor's feet. 'Have patience, lord,' he wept. 'I'll pay back every penny I owe you.'

Then the emperor felt sorry for him. He forgave the governor the whole of his huge debt.

When the governor went out of the palace he met one of his servants who owed him a small sum.

'Pay your debts!' he shouted, seizing his servant.

The poor man threw himself at the governor's feet. 'Have patience, lord,' he wept. 'I'll pay back every penny I owe you.' But the governor had no mercy. He had his servant thrown into prison.

The emperor heard of this. He sent for the governor. 'You wicked servant!' he cried. 'I forgave you the huge debt you owed me. But you could not forgive your servant the tiny debt he owed you! Very well! You too can go to prison until you have paid back every penny you owe me!'

Jesus was saying in this story that God loves to forgive. But he cannot forgive you if you cannot forgive others.

Two builders

Once there were two men who each decided to build a house in a certain valley. They both set to work at about the same time.

Simon was a wise man. He knew that the most important part of a house is its foundation. He dug down in the earth until he came to solid rock. Then he began to build. Slowly his house rose up on the rock.

Jude was a foolish man. He wanted a fine-looking house. He did not bother about a foundation. He built his house on the sand. So he easily finished first. He was proud of his smart house and how quickly he had finished.

In autumn the heavy rains came in violent storms. Soon a raging torrent poured through the valley, and swirled around the two houses. Simon's house stood firm on its rock. But the floods sucked away the sands under Jude's house and the storms battered its walls. It began to totter and crumble, until it fell with a loud crash and was carried away in the flood.

'The wise man,' said Jesus, 'listens to my teaching and lives by it. His character is like the house built on rock – nothing can shake it. The foolish man hears my teaching but does not follow it. His character has no foundation. When the storms of life come he cannot stand upright.'

Stewards

A steward looked after his master's household. Everyone
knew him by the keys of his master's house which hung from
his waist. His master trusted him to care for his house and all
his other servants. When his master was away he was in
complete charge.

'What is a good steward like?' said Jesus. 'When his
master is away he acts just the same as when his master is
there. When his master returns he sees how well his steward
has looked after his household, and rewards him.'

'But what is the bad steward like? When his master goes away he says to himself: "Now I can do as I like!" He eats his master's food and drinks his wine. He beats the servants and treats them cruelly. Then, when he least expects it, his master returns and catches him out. The master treats him exactly as he deserves – giving him a good beating, and throwing him out of his house. For much is expected from a man to whom much is given.'

Each of us is a steward of God. He gives us life and talents and he trusts us to use them well. A good and faithful steward will always be busy in the service of his master, and in doing his master's will.

148

Jesus goes to Jerusalem

Jesus was going to Jerusalem for the feast of Passover, the most sacred time of the whole year. Now he was going to claim openly to be the promised Saviour of the people of God.

There were plots against Jesus in Jerusalem. News of his words and deeds had spread far and wide. The leaders of the people were worried. They met together to decide what to do about Jesus. 'What are we to do?' they said in their council. 'If we let this man Jesus go on with his teaching and healing the people will follow him. Then the Romans will get suspicious. They will suspect another rising against them. They will take away our power and rule the country themselves. They will destroy our people, and our holy temple.'

Caiaphas, the High Priest, decided what must be done. 'We cannot let our people be destroyed,' he said. 'We can only save our people by getting rid of this Jesus. That is what we must do. One man must die so that the people may live.'

Jesus knew what dangers he faced in Jerusalem. He was ready to suffer and to die to show men the love of God and to win them to him.

Jesus at Bethany

Jesus and his twelve disciples came to Bethany, a village close to Jerusalem. Jesus was staying there, for the Passover, with a family of friends. They were Martha, her sister Mary, and their brother Lazarus.

It was the custom to welcome guests by anointing their heads with cool, refreshing oil. Mary had a costly present for Jesus to show her love. It was a tiny jug made of white marble. Inside it were just a few drops of spikenard, a precious oil from faraway India. Mary broke off the neck of the little jug and let the drops of perfumed oil fall on the head of Jesus. At once the whole house was filled with its lovely fragrance.

Judas Iscariot, the disciple who looked after the money, was horrified. 'What a waste!' he said angrily. 'That oil could have been sold and the money given to the poor!' The others grumbled too.

'Let her alone!' said Jesus. 'Why do you trouble her? She has done something beautiful to show her love for me. You will always have poor people you can help. But you will not always have me. It is as if she knows that I am going to die, and is anointing my body before the burial. Truly, I tell you, her loving deed will never be forgotten.'

151

Jesus chooses an ass

On the first day of the Passover week Jesus sent two disciples ahead to the village of Bethphage, just outside Jerusalem.
'As you enter the village you will see an ass tied to the railings by the road,' Jesus told them. 'Untie the ass and bring it to me. If anyone asks what you are doing just say: "The master needs it and will send it back as soon as he has finished with it."'

When the two disciples reached Bethphage it was exactly as Jesus had said. For Jesus was borrowing the ass from a friend,

and he quite understood the message Jesus had sent.

Why did Jesus choose an ass to ride into Jerusalem? Asses were common, of course. Most people rode on them, for they were safe and sure-footed. But Jesus had a special reason. It was in the sacred writings. A messenger of God had said, long before: 'Behold, O Jerusalem! Your king comes to you humbly, riding on an ass.'

Kings rode on horses. So did soldiers. So horses were signs of power and of war. But there was nothing proud or warlike about a lowly ass. It was humble and peaceful. Jesus chose an ass to show that he was the king, promised long before. The promised Saviour was coming to Jerusalem.

Jesus enters Jerusalem

The disciples threw cloaks over the ass to make a saddle for Jesus. They walked beside him as the ass picked its way along the road to the walls of Jerusalem. There were other pilgrims from Galilee on the road and they recognised Jesus. Soon there was an excited and joyful crowd around him. Some people cut down branches from the palm trees to wave in his honour. Others spread garments in the road to make a royal way for Jesus. There were many shouts of 'Hosanna', the cry of joy and praise to God. And the people joined in the song: 'Blessed is he who comes in the name of the Lord.'

It was a happy and joyful little procession of pilgrims from
Galilee. But there were Pharisees, devout men, standing by
the road. They were disgusted by the noisy and excited
crowd around Jesus. 'Master!' they called to Jesus. 'Tell your
disciples to behave themselves!'

Jesus answered them: 'I tell you that if they remained
silent the very stones in the road would cry out!'

So Jesus entered the holy city. His eyes filled with tears and
his heart with sorrow. 'O Jerusalem, Jerusalem,' Jesus wept.
'How often I would have gathered your people to me, as a hen
gathers her chicks under her wings! If only you would come
to me and find your peace in me.'

155

The Last Supper

The most solemn part of Passover week was the sacred meal on Friday. But Jesus knew that his time was short. Supper on Thursday evening with his disciples would be their sacred meal. It would be their last supper together, too.

During the meal Jesus took one of the flat, round loaves of bread and blessed it. He broke it in pieces and gave a piece to each disciple. 'Take and eat,' he said. 'This bread is my body which is given for you. Do this to remember me.' Then he took a large cup of wine and blessed it. He passed it round for each one to drink. 'Drink of this,' Jesus said. 'This wine is my blood which is shed for you. Do this to remember me.'

During the meal one of the disciples, Judas Iscariot, went out. The Chief Priests wanted to arrest Jesus quietly, and Judas knew where he would be alone. So they agreed to pay him thirty pieces of silver for betraying Jesus.

After supper Jesus led his disciples out of the city. As they walked he said to them: 'All of you will turn against me this night.'

Peter burst out: 'Even if they all turn against you, I never will!'

Jesus answered him: 'Truly I tell you that this very night before the cock crows twice you will deny me three times.'

157

Judas betrays Jesus

Jesus led his disciples out of Jerusalem to a quiet garden named Gethsemane, which means oil-press. It was there that olives from trees higher up the hill were pressed to make olive oil.

Jesus took his three closest disciples, Peter and James and John, into a lonely part of the garden. He was very troubled and in deep distress. 'My soul is full of sorrow,' Jesus said. 'Stay here with me and keep watch.' He went a little way from them and fell to the ground. 'Father,' they heard him cry in agony, 'all things are possible to you. Take this suffering from me. But let your will be done, not mine.'

The three disciples could not share the agony of Jesus for their eyes were heavy. Twice Jesus came and found them asleep. Then he woke them a third time. 'The hour has come,' he said. 'Rise and let us go. My betrayer is here.'

A band of men, armed with swords and clubs, were coming. They were led by Judas Iscariot. He came straight up to Jesus. 'Hail, master!' he said in a loud voice, betraying Jesus with the kiss of friendship.

That was the signal to the servants of the Chief Priests. They seized Jesus, bound his hands, and led him away. His disciples fled.

Peter denies Jesus

The armed men took Jesus to the house of Caiaphas, the High Priest. Members of the council were there too, for time was short. Saturday was the Sabbath Day when no work of any kind could be done. So Caiaphas and the council had to get rid of Jesus during Friday.

Peter and another disciple followed the armed men. The maidservant at the door knew the other disciple and let them both in. She looked hard at Peter. 'You were with this Jesus too,' she said, recognising him.

Peter answered quickly without thinking: 'I don't know him!' Somewhere a cock crowed.

Peter stood at the back of the hall in the shadows. But it was a cold night and he moved closer to the fire where the servants were keeping warm.

The maidservant, chatting with her friends, noticed Peter. 'This man was one of them too,' she said, pointing to him.

'I don't know the man!' Peter burst out quickly.

'She's quite right,' said another servant. 'I can tell by your speech that you come from Galilee.'

'I swear I don't know the man you're talking about!' Peter cried.

It was now almost dawn, and a cock could be heard
crowing. Suddenly Peter remembered the words of Jesus:
'Before the cock crows twice you will deny me three times.'
He realised what he had done. He rushed out of the hall,
threw himself on the ground, and cried his heart out.

The death of Jesus

Caiaphas the High Priest had paid people to lie about Jesus. But they could not even agree among themselves. Then he spoke to Jesus. 'Are you the promised Saviour?' he demanded.

'I am,' said Jesus.

'Blasphemy!' cried Caiaphas to the members of the council. 'What is your verdict?'

'Guilty!' they all cried.

Blasphemy was speaking against God, mocking him. The penalty in the sacred law was death. But only the Roman governor, Pontius Pilate, could pass sentence of death. The Chief Priests had to get Pilate to sentence Jesus.

When Pilate heard that the Chief Priests had an important prisoner he acted quickly, for he could not risk a riot in the crowded city. Jesus was brought before his judgement-seat. The Chief Priests made false charges against Jesus, saying that he claimed to be a king. Pilate soon saw that Jesus was no wild rebel against the Romans. But the Chief Priests and their followers went on shouting for the death of Jesus. Then Pilate signed the order for Jesus to be put to death on a cross.

Jesus was mocked by the soldiers, beaten with whips, and made to carry part of his cross out to Skull Hill. He was nailed to the cross, and hung there between two thieves. It was nine o'clock in the morning. He died at about three o'clock in the afternoon.

Mary in the garden

Joseph of Arimathea and his friend Nicodemus were secret disciples of Jesus. Joseph went boldly to Pilate and got his permission to bury the body of Jesus. It had to be done quickly, before the Sabbath Day began at sunset.

Joseph owned a garden near Skull Hill. In it was a tomb, cut out of the rock, for himself and his family. Joseph and Nicodemus had no time for a proper burial. They wrapped the body of Jesus in white burial-sheets, laid it in the new tomb, and rolled down the heavy stone which guarded it.

Mary from Magdala, and another woman disciple of Jesus, had watched them. When the Sabbath Day was over they went to the tomb to embalm the body of Jesus with spices. They were astonished to find the stone rolled back. They hurried to tell the disciples. They ran to the tomb and went inside. There was no trace of the body of Jesus.

Mary stayed in the garden when they had gone. She was weeping bitterly and saw through her tears someone standing there.

'Why are you weeping? Who are you looking for?' the stranger asked.

'Oh sir,' Mary cried, thinking him to be the gardener, 'if you have taken him away please tell me where he is, so that I can give him proper burial.'

'Mary,' said the stranger softly. It was the voice she knew so well.

'Master!' she cried joyfully, throwing herself at his feet.

'Don't stay here,' said Jesus, gently, 'but go and tell my disciples'.

In the upper room

The disciples of Jesus met together in the upper room where they had had their last supper with him. The door was bolted and barred, for they were afraid. The Chief Priests had got rid of Jesus. They might hunt out his disciples too.

They were terrified when Jesus suddenly appeared before them. He spoke to them. 'Why are you so troubled? See my hands and my feet. A ghost does not have flesh and bones as I have.' Then Jesus told them that they were to spread the kingdom of God among men.

Thomas, one of the disciples, was not with them that evening. When he came back they told him how Jesus had appeared to them.

'I don't believe it,' said Thomas. 'I won't believe it unless I see him myself and touch him.'

Some nights later Thomas was with the other disciples in the upper room. The door was still barred. Suddenly Jesus appeared to them. 'Peace be with you,' he said. Then he turned to Thomas and stretched out his hands. 'See my hands,' he said to Thomas. 'Touch me, and believe in me.'

'My Lord and my God,' Thomas cried, falling to his knees.

'You believe in me because you have seen me,' said Jesus. 'How blessed are those who have not seen me and yet believe in me.'

The day of Pentecost

Jesus appeared to his disciples for the last time at Bethany.
'The spirit of God will come upon you,' he said. 'Then you
will be filled with power and will spread the Good News to the
ends of the earth.' Suddenly the cloud of the glory of God
shone around Jesus. When it was gone they saw him no more.

Then came the feast of Pentecost, fifty days after the
Passover. The disciples and followers of Jesus were gathered
in the upper room. Suddenly the hot morning sun seemed like
fire, setting their hearts alight. The morning breeze was like a
hurricane, blowing new life into them. And they were all
filled with power – the power of the Spirit of God.

The disciples rushed down from the upper room into the

street. A crowd quickly gathered. At once Peter proclaimed the Good News of Jesus. 'Jesus of Nazareth, put to death on the cross, has been raised up by God! We are his witnesses! He is the promised Saviour!'

Many people were greatly moved by this message. 'What shall we do?' they asked.

'Change your hearts,' said Peter. 'Be baptized in the name of Jesus. Then your sins will be forgiven, and you will receive the Spirit of God.'

That day three thousand people were baptized and gave their hearts and lives to Jesus. It was the birthday of his church – the new people of God.

Peter the leader

One day Peter and John were going into the temple. A lame man lay there asking for money.

'I have no gold or silver,' said Peter. 'But what I have I give you. In the name of Jesus – walk!'

A crowd soon gathered as the man danced with joy for his cure. Peter proclaimed the Good News to them. But then the temple guards came and imprisoned Peter and John.

The next day members of the council met to try Peter and John, just as they had met to try Jesus. They ordered the disciples to stop their preaching, and threatened them.

'You must decide whether we should listen to you or to God,' said Peter. 'We cannot help telling what we have seen and heard.'

Again Peter and the disciples were brought before the council.

'We gave you strict orders to stop your preaching,' said the High Priest.

'We must obey God, not men,' said Peter. The members of the council were furious and wanted to kill them.

But a wise teacher named Gamaliel said: 'Do not persecute these men. If their teaching is just a craze it will soon die. But if it should come from God you might be fighting against God himself.'

The council took his advice. The disciples were beaten and ordered not to speak in the name of Jesus.

The disciples went out, glad to have suffered for their master. And every day they proclaimed the Good News of Jesus.

Paul the missionary

Paul was a Pharisee, living strictly by the sacred law. He hated the followers of Jesus. Some of them fled to the Roman city of Damascus. Paul went after them to bring them back as prisoners.

Paul hurried along the road to Damascus in the glaring sun. Suddenly light blazed around him and he fell down. He heard a voice saying: 'Paul, why do you persecute me?'

'Who are you?' Paul whispered.

'I am Jesus whom you are persecuting. Rise up and go into the city, and there you will be told what you must do.'

The shock had blinded Paul and he had to be led into Damascus by his companions. But there he was baptized, his sight came back, and he was filled with the Spirit of God.

At once Paul began proclaiming Jesus as the Saviour. He became leader of the followers of Jesus in the great city of Antioch. It was there that they were given a nickname – Christians. For they believed that Jesus was the Christ, the promised Saviour.

From Antioch Paul set out on his travels as a Christian missionary. In every town he visited he left a 'church' – a group of people 'belonging to the Lord'. He wrote letters to them which we can still read in the Bible. So the Good News of Jesus spread far and wide through the work of Paul the missionary.

Peter and Paul at Rome

Paul the missionary was sometimes ill on his travels. In one town a Greek doctor named Luke came to treat him. Luke became a Christian and travelled with Paul on his journeys. Luke collected memories of Jesus and wrote them down in his *Gospel*, that is, a book of Good News. Then he wrote a history book called *The Acts of the Apostles*. It describes the lives of Peter the leader and Paul the missionary as they spread the Good News of Jesus.

Paul's enemies had him arrested at Jerusalem. He was sent to Rome to be tried before the emperor. Paul had to wait two years for his trial. He lived in his own house, but there was always a Roman soldier to guard him. The leaders of the churches came to Paul, and he sent them on journeys which he could not make himself.

Paul wrote many letters too. One was to a leader named Timothy. 'Only Luke is with me,' Paul wrote. 'Come to me as soon as you can. Bring Mark with you for he is helpful to me. Bring my warm cloak and my books with you too.'

Paul knew that he had not long to live. 'I have fought a good fight,' he wrote. 'I have kept faith with Jesus. Now I am ready to go, and to live with him for ever.' Paul was tried by the Emperor Nero and he was put to death.

Peter also went to Rome, and he too was put to death there. Today the great church of St. Peter stands on the place where he was buried.

Peter and Paul had spread the Good News of Jesus from Jerusalem to the mighty city of Rome. Now it could spread all through the Roman Empire and throughout the world.

Plan of Jerusalem

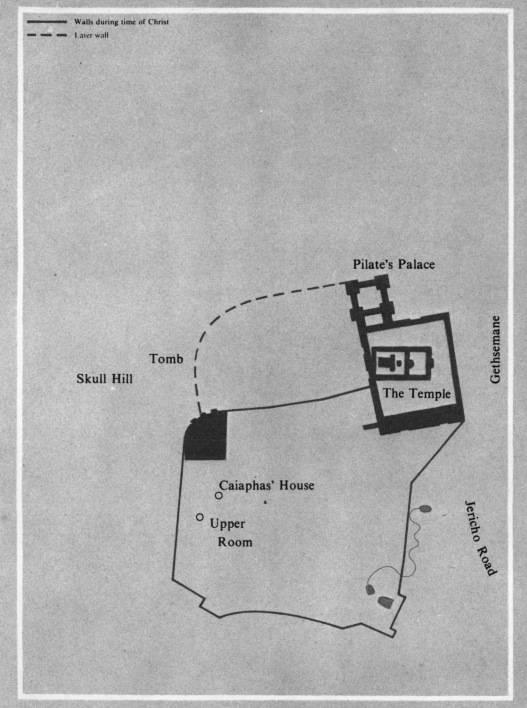

Walls during time of Christ

Later wall

Pilate's Palace

Gethsemane

Tomb

Skull Hill

The Temple

Caiaphas' House

Upper
Room

Jericho Road